Evaluation and Implementation of Distance Learning: Technologies, Tools and Techniques

France Belanger, Ph.D.
Virginia Polytechnic Institute and State University, USA

Dianne H. Jordan, Ph.D.
Booz Allen & Hamilton, Inc., USA

IDEA GROUP PUBLISHING
Hershey USA • London UK

Senior Editor:	Mehdi Khosrowpour
Managing Editor:	Jan Travers
Copy Editor:	Brenda Zboray Klinger
Typesetter:	Tamara Gillis
Cover Design:	Connie Peltz
Printed at:	BookCrafters

Published in the United States of America by
    Idea Group Publishing
    1331 E. Chocolate Avenue
    Hershey PA 17033-1117
    Tel: 717-533-8845
    Fax: 717-533-8661
    E-mail: jtravers@idea-group.com
    Website: http://www.idea-group.com

and in the United Kingdom by
    Idea Group Publishing
    3 Henrietta Street
    Covent Garden
    London WC2E 8LU
    Tel: 171-240 0856
    Fax: 171-379 0609
    http://www.eurospan.co.uk

Library of Congress Cataloging-in-Publication Data

Belanger, France, 1963-
    Evaluation and implementation of distance learning : technologies, tools and techniques / France Belanger, Dianne H. Jordan.
       p. cm.
    Includes bibliographical references and index.
    ISBN 1-878289-63-2 (paper)
       1. Distance education--Computer-assisted instructions. 2. Instructional systems--Design. 3. Education technology. I. Jordan, Dianne H., 1950-II. Title.

LC5803.C65 B45 2000   99-047580

British Cataloguing in Publication Data
A Cataloguing in Publication record for this book is available from the British Library.

To Pierre, for your unrelenting support...
-France

For Eamon and Brendan Jordan
-Dianne

NEW from Idea Group Publishing

Evaluation and Implementation of Distance Learning: Technologies, Tools and Techniques

Table of Contents

Chapter I

Introduction

Since the dawn of human history when humans began living and working together, training and education have played a critical part in the evolution of culture and society. One of the oldest forms of training is apprenticeship, where apprentices learned their craft by working for and being mentored by their masters, learning their craft until they achieved mastery of that craft. Before the era of writing, education involved teaching survival skills to youth such as gathering food, building weapons and shelters, and teaching social skills about behavioral norms in communities. Beginning in the middle ages, centers of learning developed around the physical location of the teacher and the library of books in the scholar's possession. In the age of computers and networks, we have finally broken through these physical limitations of time and space.

The 20th century has seen the creation and evolution of technologies beyond imagination a century ago. The computer enabled the digital presentation of knowledge, and increased the speed with which information can be captured and processed. Communication technologies made possible the storage, transfer, and sharing of information across vast distances and different time zones. These technologies led to new alternatives for providing education and training in ways not possible just a few decades ago. In particular, improvements in telecommunication technologies paved the way for development of new instructional technologies and communication tools that can deliver knowledge without the limitations imposed by traditional learning environments. At the dawn of the 21st century, we are witnessing unprecedented growth in the number of commercial, governmental, and educational institutions planning or implementing some form of distance learning.

The number of learners participating in distance learning environments is expected to exceed 3 million by the year 2000 (Gubernick and Ebeling, 1997). One well-known example of a successful distance education program is the Open University in Britain, which is nationally supported and has over 133,000 students taking courses exclusively on-line (Encarta®, 1998). The University started in 1969 and used television as a delivery mechanism. It then evolved to use computer-based training and more recently digital libraries and multimedia facilities. Currently, there are nationally supported open universities in over twenty countries worldwide. In addition, there are over 100 universities that offer more than 2,500 courses over the Internet (LaRose, Gregg, and Eastin, 1998). The reasons for the rapid growth of distance learning in recent years include (Race and Brown, 1995):

- Lower cost of computer hardware, software, and telecommunications services;
- Younger generation familiar with computers and the Internet;
- Younger generation has better keyboarding skills and less fear of technology;
- Better access to computers in the general population;
- More pleasing users interfaces (including multimedia).

As we enter the 21st century, organizations in the private and public sectors face increased financial and business challenges. These challenges have created an imperative for distance learning as a practical solution that can:

- lower the costs of education and training per learner;
- increase education and training opportunities for all knowledge workers who work with and produce value from information,

rather than from products of physical labor;
- provide lifelong learning opportunities for people of all ages, lifestyles, capabilities, and financial situations.

Objectives of the Book

This book focuses on the dominant processes, techniques, and tools that have been used to successfully plan, implement, and operate distance learning projects. It will be informative and useful for professionals and educators who are interested in preparing themselves for the transition from traditional learning to the emerging distance learning environment. The three main goals of this book are:

1. To provide a framework for understanding important theoretical concepts that must be applied when considering distance learning. Distance learning technologies allow instructor and learners to be separated by physical distance and/or separated in time, and where learning may or may not take place simultaneously with other learners.
2. To discuss the latest advances in educational technologies, tools, and techniques, and what infrastructure capabilities are required to support them in the organization.
3. To provide a methodology for analyzing and assessing the content and delivery of traditional classroom-based instruction to determine whether, and to what extent, the content can be converted to one or more distance learning technologies.

Managers, educators, or professionals who are assigned to implement distance learning projects are faced with an overwhelming task if they believe that they must take all of their course offerings and convert them completely to distance learning. While this is an implied assumption in most of the distance learning literature, the reality is that distance learning conversion is not an all-or-nothing experience. The technologies, tools, and procedures presented in this book can be used in three ways to evolve progressively towards a comprehensive distance learning environment. The first is *technology insertion* where instructional technologies are embedded in the traditional classroom environment. The second is *combined delivery* where part of a course is delivered via the traditional classroom and part of the course is delivered via distance learning tools. Third and most extensive is *total conversion* where traditional classroom education and training is entirely converted to one or more distance learning formats. The material presented in this book is appropriate for all of three approaches to distance learning.

Organization of the Book

This chapter provides an overview of distance learning, including definitions of concepts and terms, and an overview of learning variables in the distributed learning environment. Chapter two presents an in-depth review of the learning theories and variables that apply to distance learning. Chapter three provides a detailed review and analysis of the educational technologies and tools used in distance education and training. Chapters four through six are dedicated to analysis, design, and implementation of a distance learning project. In chapter four, the reader is presented with methodologies and design considerations for evaluating existing course materials and infrastructures in preparation for conversion to distance learning. Chapter five discusses instructional systems development considerations and tools for converting current course material to distance learning formats. Chapter six provides guidelines for implementing and evaluating distance learning courses and programs. Finally, Chapter seven presents three fictional case studies outlining the evaluation and implementation processes performed for the conversion of training courses to distance learning.

The Need For Distance Learning

Despite initial concerns that distance learning might lower the quality of instruction, studies show that its benefits are clear and demonstrable, and many forms of distance learning are quickly gaining acceptance. There are several reasons for this growth. First, distance learning opens up new opportunities for students that might otherwise be excluded from participating in the learning process. These potential learners include individuals with limited mobility because of handicaps or obligations, such as child care or elderly care, or those living and working in remote areas where such education has never been available. Second, distance learning allows institutions to educate a larger number of students with relatively fewer instructors, thus providing a cost-effective method of delivering higher education. Third, learners have the opportunity to pursue lifelong learning

Table 1.1 Expected Benefits of Distance Learning

Learners	Instructors	Institutions
• Increased flexibility • Increased access to learning • Increased choice of institution • Lifelong learning • Access to remote experts • Increased performance • Increased promotion potential • Increased compensation • Better marketability	• Increased participation • Broader time frame to deliver courses	• Increased number of learners • Increased variety of learners • Competitive advantage • Decreased costs • More scheduling flexibility • Less classroom requirements • Increased employee satisfaction • Reduced turnover • Shorter training time

after graduation regardless of lifestyle or location. These benefits have led many higher educational institutions to implement some distance learning classes even if on an experimental basis. As a consequence, society in general may benefit from an overall increase in literacy through greater access to education. It is not surprising that in the United States alone, 62 % of public four-year institutions offered some courses over the Internet in 1995—an increase of 150 % over 1992 (National Center for Educational Statistics, 1997).

For commercial and governmental institutions the focus is not as much on education as it is on training. Training is different from education in that it involves job-specific learning objectives and activities, and the content is specific to the performance of the job. Corporations offer training to employees to ensure that they remain current with changes and innovations in their industry or field. Distance training provides these organizations with opportunities to let employees update their skills while remaining at their workplace or their home. For employees, training impacts their ability to find jobs, their work performance, their rewards and compensation, and could even affect their promotion potential (Whalen and Wright, 1998). This tends to increase the overall satisfaction of workers with their job and, therefore, decrease turnover rates. Some of these benefits are highlighted in Table 1.1.

For corporations, a key benefit of implementing distance training is cost savings. Providing the training in the employee's normal work location substantially reduces travel costs. In addition, employees remain productive by taking courses without incurring the additional time required for travel and from reduction in overall time spent on training. One manager from Hewlett-Packard Corporation, in a personal conversation with one of the authors, mentioned that "we cannot afford to send them [new employees] to six months of training [anymore]". Distance learning offers companies the opportunity to maintain their employees' expertise as the company's business needs, as well as technology, rapidly evolve. Several corporations and government agencies have published statistics highlighting the financial benefits of distance training. For example, the Safeguard and Security Central Training of the Department of Energy in New Mexico cut the per person costs of training by 200% using satellite-based interactive television costs (Schaaf, 1997). Similar statistics have been published for Budget Rent-A Car, the Oklahoma Department of Human Services, and others who have implemented distance learning technologies (Schaaf, 1997). Overall, distance learning is increasingly becoming an attractive alternative in industry and government, particularly when they have employees that are "widely distributed geographically, or when a large number of [learners] need to take the same course" (Whalen and Wright, 1998).

Defining Concepts

Distance learning can be thought of as education or training delivered to individuals who are geographically dispersed or separated by physical distance from the instructor using computer and telecommunication facilities. Historically, the precursor of technology-based distance learning was correspondence education, which started in Europe and the United States in the mid 19th century. It was established to provide education to those who could not attend traditional classroom environments, and used the postal system as a delivery mechanism. Beginning in the middle of the 20th century and continuing today, television began playing a role in providing distance education courses. For example, the Public Broadcasting Corporation in the United States presents courses that are taken by students in over 2,000 institutions. Individuals can enroll and complete courses from home. Recently, educational delivery to mass audiences based on correspondence and television courses have found new competition as newer information systems and communication technologies have emerged. The most prominent of these delivery vehicles as we enter the new millennium is the Internet, which has generated a new phenomenon of the virtual learning environment. Some companies specialize in offering training over the Internet, such as the Virtual University for Small and Medium Sized Enterprises (http:// www.vusme.org) or the Infobahn Webschool (http://www.i-bahn.com/web/index.html).

What is so unique about the Internet that led to an explosion of distance learning programs? First, when discussing the Internet, one must be clear that it is not the Internet per se but its graphical interface, the Web browser, that has spurred tremendous increase in the use of the Internet worldwide. The Web browser is easy to use. While Web browser interfaces differ slightly between products, the products all have similar functionality such that users can easily navigate through information content posted on the Internet. The universal appeal and ease of use of the Web browser is the reason that many institutions deliver their distance learning courses via the Internet or their organizational intranet. The second major reason for the increased use of the Internet for distance learning is that it is a relatively inexpensive medium. Most students can connect to the Internet without additional charge (although the cost of Internet access may be embedded in their college fees). For an instructor, material can be posted and maintained with ease using Web authoring tools. On the other hand, at the enterprise level, the costs of implementing a large distance learning program may be substantial. Infrastructure upgrades may be required, and initial investments of instructor time, developer time, and software costs must be incurred until they can be offset by savings after implementation. Consideration of costs and the value of potential benefits are key factors in the decision-making process for distance learning implementation, and they will be covered in Chapter four.

A major problem confronting researchers interested in studying distance learning or professionals interested in evaluating and implementing distance learning is that the literature presents a wide variety of distance learning terms. For example, the terms open university, open learning, distance education, distance training, distance learning, distance teaching, virtual learning, virtual university, computer mediated education, computer assisted instruction, computer mediated training, open learning environments, tele-learning, asynchronous learning networks, or Web-based instructional systems all refer to some form of distance learning. Table 1.2 provides definitions for some of the terms found in the literature.

As the reader will quickly realize, the plethora of distance learning terms that describe related or similar phenomena makes it more difficult to absorb the relevant literature on the subject. We will help clarify some critical differences between the terms found in Table 1.2 by highlighting three problem areas in the definition of distance learning. First, there is an important difference in the learning environment, mission, and purpose of training and education, which continues in distance training and distance education environments. Second, the differences between distance teaching and distance learning are explained. Finally, differences exist between the levels of technology usage in the various distance education and training environments.

Table 1.2 Definitions for Some Distance Education and Training Terms

Term	Definition	Source
Asynchronous learning networks	"a teaching and learning environment located within a Computer Mediated Communication system designed for anytime/anyplace use through computer networks"	Hiltz, 1997
Collaborative telelearning	"collaborative learning among non-proximate team members"	Alavi et al., 1995
Distance Education	"variety of educational programs and activities... [where] the learner and teacher are physically separate but...efforts are made...to overcome this separation using a variety of media"	UNESCO, 1987
Distance Learning	"category of training which is technology-based and where the instructor and students are separated geographically"	Whalen and Wright, 1998
Distance Teaching	"family of instructional methods in which the teaching behaviors are executed apart from the learning behaviors...so that communication between the teacher and the learner must be facilitated by print, mechanical and other devices"	Moore, 1973
Flexible Learning	"all those situations where learners have some say in how, where, and when learning takes place"	Ellington, 1997
Technology-mediated distance learning	"learning involving the implementation of information, computing, and communication technology applications"	Webster and Hackley, 1997

Distance Training and Distance Education

By its nature, training is focused on the development and performance of specific tasks or skills. In the work environment, training is provided so that the knowledge gained can be applied to the performance of job-related actions and behaviors. Training tends to be more job or company specific and involves the acquisition of job-related skills by employees. Even generic training, such as learning computer skills, is usually offered to employees in positions requiring those skills, or who aspire to such jobs. By contrast, education is oriented towards more generalized and abstract knowledge that may or may not be directly tied to specific tasks or actions. For example, a course entitled the "Management of Information Systems" will not address specific tasks or a specific job for any one person but will cover the important concepts, issues, and problems encountered in the management of information technologies. Thus, it can be applied by the student to any number of specific job situations but requires higher order analytical skills of the student to employ theses general concepts for specific use in the workplace.

Distance Teaching and Distance Learning

While the terms teaching and learning seem to be used interchangeably when attached to the word distance, they really refer to two different concepts. Distance teaching should be viewed from the instructors' side and involves delivering education or training material while not being physically present at the same location as the students. Distance learning, on the other hand, should be viewed from the learners' perspective. It is closely tied to distance teaching, but learning may not occur in the distance environment if barriers exist from the learners' point of view, such as difficulty in using the technology, or lack of instructor interaction when answering questions.

Defining Distance and Distributed Learning

In light of the differences that exist between the various definitions, it can be useful to map them to a framework that compares time and place separation between learners, learners and instructors, and learner and learning resources, as presented in Figure 1.1. Chapter two will discuss learning variables more in depth, including the role of asynchronous and synchronous learning modes in distance learning.

As can be seen from Figure 1.1, and as previously discussed,

Figure 1.1 Time/Place Framework for Technology Supported Distance Learning

	Synchronous (Same Time)	**Asynchronous (Different Time)**
Same Place Place	**TRADITIONAL LEARNING** (Classroom) Face-to-face meetings with Technology Insertion (CAI using computers, videos, or Web-based material in PC labs).	**ASYNCHRONOUS DISTANCE LEARNING** (Using Learning Centers or Labs) Learning at own pace in own time within organization's facilities (CBT with CD-ROM, disks or tapes).
Different Place	**REAL-TIME DISTANCE LEARNING** Live courses via high speed data links such as LANs, Satellites and the Internet (Communication Supported WBT, Teleconferencing, and VTT)	**DISTRIBUTED LEARNING** Learning at own pace in their own time, independent of geographic location (Videotaped courses, WBT, and CBT). Can incorporate aspects of the other quadrants.

technology can be used in a variety of ways to implement varying levels of distance education and training. Particular attention should be placed on the fourth quadrant, which defines *distributed* learning. So far, much of the discussion has been concentrated on distance, where the learner is remote from the instructor. Several researchers will state that today the trend is towards distributed learning, where the learner is not only separated physically from the instructor (and other learners), but also is learning at his or her own pace at a time that is convenient to him or her. Being able to teach and to learn irrespective of time and place is increasingly being facilitated through Web-based courses. Quadrant four, distributed learning, can include both real-time distance learning (DL) and asynchronous DL. Therefore, from this point onward in the book, the term distance learning will be used to refer to both distance education and distance training (unless specifically indicated). Advantages and disadvantages of each approach listed in Figure 1.1 will be discussed at length in chapter three.

Evaluating Distance Learning

As DL gains momentum and popularity, some of the important questions asked by managers interested in implementing such programs include:

- What do we get out of our investments in DL?
- Will our employees be better trained by using DL technologies? Or will they be as well trained as compared with our traditional training environments?
- What can we do to increase the likelihood that our DL programs will be successful?

Similarly, the administrator and teacher from an educational institution may ask questions about a DL program:

- How do we evaluate the success of our DL programs?
- Will the students be benefited if they learn via DL instead of regular classroom courses?
- Will DL allow us to increase our student throughput without increasing costs?

These questions reflect two sets of important issues. First, what are the determinants of a successful DL program? And second, how do we measure success (or failure) of the program? These questions will be investigated in depth in chapter six, which looks at implementation and evaluation of distance education and training courses.

An appropriately planned and well executed DL program can have beneficial effects on the organization and the learner. In order to reap these benefits, we must prepare ourselves as learners and educators, and we must prepare our institutions for the changes that will ensue.

Chapter II

Learning Variables in Distance Learning

Chapter one introduced distance learning definitions and concepts as applied to education and training. An important consideration when choosing among DL technologies is the potential effect of DL technology use on the learning experience. This chapter provides a discussion of key learning variables in the learning process and outcome. These variables characterize and differentiate the DL technologies and are used in the course evaluation and media selection process. After the learning variables are presented in this chapter, the instructional technologies are discussed and evaluated in chapter three. Finally, readers will find the details of the screening process for distance learning described in depth in chapter four.

Learning is so important that a number of theories have been developed to explain its constructs, its processes, and its outcomes. The most traditional model is the objectivist model where learners have an objective reality to learn with knowledge that is transferred by an expert (instructor or teacher) (Jonassen, 1993). This model of learning suggests that mass media would be the most important delivery method, where knowledge is sent by a subject matter expert in one-way communication to learners (receivers). The constructivist model of learning assumes that knowledge is not transferred but created (or recreated) by the learner, and the instructor is a facilitator. In this model, learners take control of the learning process (Leidner and Jarvenpaa, 1995). The use of instructional technologies in this model of learning might include computer-mediated communication technologies that focus on interpersonal (both synchronous and asynchronous) communication, feedback, and synergy. This model also lends itself to self-pacing and learner control through decision making in the learning process. Another model, the cooperative learning model, promotes interaction between learners as a way to facilitate learning. The use of instructional technologies under this model might focus on collaboration tools such as shared whiteboards and virtual workspaces.

What these models all have in common is that they all involve key elements of the instructional environment—learners, instructors, institutions, and the learning process. The remainder of this chapter discusses learning variables associated with the learning theories described above. Chapter three will provide a discussion of the technologies that support the learning process.

LEARNING OBJECTIVES

A key consideration for the success of a DL environment is whether or not, and to what degree, learning objectives can be met using different delivery technologies. Instructional methods such as lectures, tests, tutorials or quizzes can be used in both technology-supported and non-technology-supported environments. Most instructional methods are designed to successfully achieve the learning objectives of the learning module or course. Using today's advanced DL technologies it is possible to achieve these learning objectives without the presence of the instructor or without the co-location of all learners in one physical area. Each technology discussed in chapter three can, to varying degrees, achieve learning objectives. It is important to evaluate all learning objectives associated with a course or learning module before considering whether, and to what degree, DL technologies are most effectively (for cost and instructional integrity) used to achieve those objectives. Evaluating courses is an iterative process with a goal of finding the best "fit" of technologies based on learning objectives, capabilities of the technologies, and cost effectiveness.

Figure 2.1 Learning Objectives

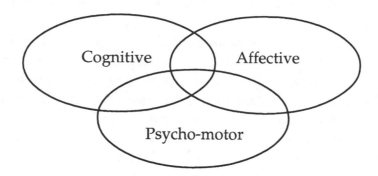

In general, there are three main learning objective categories: psycho-motor, cognitive, and affective, which are depicted in Figure 2.1. In the traditional classroom environment, learning objectives are assessed in a variety of ways, usually involving testing or evaluation of the learner's performance. For example, in many educational institutions, mid-term and final exams assess student learning at two points during the course. Written and oral assignments give an instructor the opportunity to assess each learner's performance against learning objectives in the cognitive domain. Courses with psycho-motor objectives are also assessed with performance-based tests and evaluations such as demonstrating a physical skill. Many instructors also include qualitative factors in their assessment of learners — "class participation," evidence of "motivation to learn," or other interaction between the instructor and the learner — to indicate extraordinary effort on the part of the learner. These qualitative factors could be classified as objectives in the affective domain.

Distance learning separates the instructor from the learner, and in many cases, the learner from other learners. Traditional methods of assessing learner performance may need to be replaced with a combination of DL technologies that provide the learner with the opportunity to demonstrate achievement of learning objectives, and that provide the instructor with an opportunity to assess learners' performance along the cognitive, psycho-motor, or affective domains.

Learning Objectives in the Cognitive Domain

Bloom (1956) identified six major categories of learning objectives in the cognitive domain: knowledge, comprehension, application, analysis, synthesis, and evaluation. Each category builds upon the requirements and characteristics of the one before it, and each category is further broken down into subcategories. Cognitive learning objectives are relatively easy to achieve using distance learning technologies, although the level of interactivity and media richness requirements increase as the objectives increase in complexity from knowledge through evaluation. Media Richness Theory (Daft and Lengel, 1986) describes the degree to which various communication media provide contextual cues, with face-to-face meetings being the richest medium for communication. Examples of cognitive learning objectives are presented next.

Knowledge

Knowledge involves the recall of patterns, structures, or settings, and can involve the recall of specific facts (e.g., terminology) or ways and means of dealing with those facts (e.g., trends, methodology, principles, and theories). This type of cognitive objective is satisfied with recognition and recall, and there is no required comprehension to understand the underlying phenomena. Learning content in the form of definitions and terms (often multiple-choice options in testing) is an example of knowledge objectives within the cognitive domain.

Comprehension

Comprehension is considered to be the lowest level of understanding within the cognitive domain and includes translation, interpretation (ability to grasp the material as a whole at different levels of generality) and extrapolation (determining implications, trends, or consequences of statements in the material) of the material being learned. Essay tests requiring students to integrate material from various sources are examples of methods used to evaluate comprehension.

Application

Application requires the use of generalizations or abstractions in concrete or specific situations. Abstractions may be in the form of principles, theories, or ideas which must be applied. In some distance education and training environments where technology insertion is used, learners can apply the knowledge gained in the classroom on their remote (home) computer or equipment setup (using some forms of computer- or Web-based assisted instruction). An example of an application learning objective is from one of the author's database class. Students are taught principles of database design in the classroom, which they must then apply in designing an actual real-world database using a stand-alone PC database application outside the classroom.

Analysis

Analysis requires breaking down the learning content into its basic components with an understanding of the relationship between and among components of the topic. For example, a learner may be required to analyze the elements and relationships of the components of the material in a logical way or may be required to analyze the principles by which the underlying topic is structured or organized.

Synthesis

Synthesis requires the ability to reorganize or restructure the components of the content into a whole. This may involve rearranging elements that were decomposed in analysis and recomposing them into new patterns. Learning objectives at this level require creativity in generating new knowledge, and new ways of thinking about existing ideas.

Evaluation

Evaluation involves quantitative and qualitative judgements about the value of the material and its ability to achieve its given purpose. Judgements can be made using logic and consistency as a guide (internal criteria) or with reference to other works (external criteria). Learning objectives at this level require the skills and abilities demonstrated in all the other objectives within the cognitive domain. Achieving the evaluation level in the cognitive domain of learning objectives is more difficult to measure without an instructor-led or instructor-guided learning environment because it requires grading the ability of the learner to critically evaluate the material given in the course. All doctoral-level programs of learning involve evaluation as a learning objective.

Learning Objectives in the Psycho-Motor Domain

Psycho-motor objectives focus on muscular or motor skills, manipulation of objects, or other physical activities that require neuro-muscular coordination. These objectives are most prominent in learning material related to speech, physical education, trades, operation of machinery, and technical courses for which there is a component requiring mastery of physical activity. While at first glance it seems that learning objectives in the psycho-motor domain may not be appropriate for consideration using distance learning technologies, one need only recall late night television infomercials for exercise videos, marshal art courses, and other fitness activities. Brute force is not the only focus of psycho-motor learning objectives—precision flying simulators, simulation equipment for chemistry laboratory experiments, and other tasks demanding coordination skills have been taught using distance learning technologies. For example, multimedia technologies have been successfully used to develop physical skills in hazardous environments—e.g. aircraft simulators allow students to make and learn from errors in a simulator where in real life the mistake might cost them their life. Lower level psycho-motor skills that can be useful in distance learning include typing capabilities.

Learning Objectives in the Affective Domain

Learning objectives in the affective domain are difficult to structure because the objectives focus on the learner's interests, emotions, perceptions, tone, aspirations, and degree of acceptance or rejection of the instructional content. Affective objectives outlined in Bloom's taxonomy (Krathwohl, Bloom, and Masia, 1964) range from simple attention to the more complex aspects of character and conscience. An example would be the viewing of the movie "Schindler's List" to a class studying the holocaust—the emotional impact of the movie achieves a depth of understanding about the complexities and horrors of the holocaust that is different than the presentation of material that focuses solely on cognitive objectives (concepts, terms, and definitions).

Affective learning objectives are met in two ways through the use of distance learning technologies. First, the use of multimedia technologies (audio, video, interactive text and graphics) raises the general level of interest and engagement of the student with the instructional content. The second way affective learning objectives are met in DL environments is by engaging the learner through multiple sensory organs with the instructional material. DL courses that require the learner to read material while hearing or viewing images forces him or her to use more senses than learners sitting passively in lecture-based course environments. This helps students to retain cognitive material. In other words, there is an affective aspect to the retention of cognitive material that is enhanced. There are several subcategories of learning objectives in the affective domain, which are described below.

Receiving (Attending)

This learning objective requires the learner to be aware of the existence of phenomena or stimuli. It does not require recall of those stimuli, just awareness and receptiveness to the stimuli, and attention to the stimuli. This learning objective is often achieved with toddlers when their mothers take them to the library for "reading hour." The goal is for the young toddler to achieve the ability to attend to the stimulus of the story teller. It is also, sadly, an objective that is difficult to achieve with children who suffer from autism. With older learners, this objective may be achieved through practice to develop apprecia-tion for musical elements, for example.

Responding

Responding to learning phenomena requires a commitment by the learner to participate in the learning process through willingness to respond or obtaining satisfaction through affective response to a learning experience. For example, classes designed to increase the motivation of learners to develop and use effective study skills must get them to respond positively to reinforcement for learning these skills.

Valuing

The concept of valuing can only be measured in behavior that reflects acceptance or preference for a value, or commitment to a value—"internalization" of value. For example, a learning objective for a class in American Government might be to internalize the values upon which our democracy was founded—e.g., free speech, indi-vidual rights, freedom of religion. Beyond a cognitive objective of learning places, and dates of important events in American history, or being able to apply aspects of Constitutional law to current events, an objective (particularly in childhood education) may include the acceptance and adoption of "American values."

Organization

Organization involves understanding the interrelationships among different values and being able to organize them into a system of values. This requires the ability to conceptualize a value before being able to organize it within a system of values. An example would be to be able to discuss the elements of an ethical standard, based on philosophical criteria for good and evil.

Characterization by a Value or Value Complex

Learning objectives in the affective domain at this level require the individual to act in a consistent manner with the internalized values— it involves generalization of situations in the external world in order to make judgements about issues, situations, and consequences that are consistent with his/her value system. An example would be the ability to articulate a value or belief within the context of a larger philosophical or spiritual framework.

INTERACTIVITY

Interactivity is a key element of the learning environment. In a keynote address to the 21st annual conference on Interactive Systems for Training, Education, and Job Performance, Roger Schank of the Cognitive Arts Corporation talked about natural learning processes that a two-year old child employs—largely based on curiosity, exploration, and trial-and-error. He spoke of how children as well as adults learn more effectively through making mistakes, and how DL technologies can be employed effectively by enabling learners to make errors without embarrassment or negative consequences. The cooperative model of learning actually assumes that interaction between a learner and other learners is the way learning is promoted (Slavin, 1990).

In the world of distance learning technology, there is a slight variation in the meaning of the term interactivity, where the term includes the interactive properties or capabilities of the media as well as the degree of engagement between the learner and the instructional content. The concept of interactivity also extends beyond the realms of interactive properties of the instructional technologies to include interpersonal communication between learners and between learners and instructors.

There are several important reasons to promote some or all types of interactions in distance learning courses. Some of the reasons suggested by instructors and participants alike include the following:

- Decreases the sense of isolation of individuals involved in distance courses.
- Increases the flexibility of individuals to adapt to new conditions.
- Increases the variety of experiences individual learners are exposed to, such as multicultural environments, broader age range of learners, or greater overall expertise of all learners combined.
- Interaction may be a requirement for some types of courses, such as journalism or interpersonal communications.
- Allows more senses to be used in the learning process (besides passive listening).

Interactive Properties of the Communication Channel

Individual learners involved in DL programs must typically use some communication medium to complete their course requirements. The concept of interactivity is grounded in communication theory, which has evolved from early mathematical models such as Shannon's (1948) model of one-way linear communication (transmitter-medium-receiver). Berlo's model of communication (1960) included the concept of communication fidelity, which described the degree of effectiveness of the communication in achieving the purpose of the sender. Fidelity was affected by four source-related factors: communication skills, attitudes, knowledge level, and position within a sociocultural system.

Media Richness and Social Presence Theories were later proposed to explain the relative richness of communication media in supporting interactions between individuals (Daft and Lengel, 1986; Walther, 1992 and 1995). The basic premise of the theories is that each medium is said to have some interactive communication properties that make it better (or worse) at supporting certain types of communication between individuals. For example, in distance and distributed learning environments, interactive videos between instructors and learners provide a richer environment, simulating face-to-face interactions and providing more cues to the interacting parties, such as looks of non-comprehension, boredom or excitement in learners' faces as a particular topic is being taught. The capability of promoting interaction of each instructional technology will be discussed in chapter three.

Interaction between Instructor and Learner

Interaction between instructors and learners has always existed. What is different in the DL environment is that the instructor is separated from the learner by time and/or space, as compared with face-to-face interaction of the traditional classroom environment. DL technologies vary in their inherent abilities to transmit communication richness in the interaction between instructor and learners. As chapter three describes, some distance learning technologies are synchronous, i.e., they enable instructor and learner to communicate in real time; others are asynchronous, i.e., they allow for communication but in a sequential fashion with some time lapse between interactions.

Recent communication scholars such as Williams, Rice, and Rogers (1988) reach back to Wiener's cybernetic model of communication, which incorporated the concept of feedback loops in communication. This concept of communication was largely ignored in its day because it was not applicable to mass media, which was characterized by one-way communication (such as radio and broadcast television). Feedback loops are especially important in DL where instructors are geographically separated from learners. Instructors need feedback from learners to ensure comprehension of material and to obtain information on their own performance in delivering the material. Learners, on the other hand, need feedback from the instructor on their achievement in the classes they take. Communication feedback is highly relevant in a discussion of modern communication media because of the two-way (asynchronous and synchronous) capability of computer-mediated communications technologies. Williams, Rice, and Rogers defined interactivity as "the degree to which participants in a communication process have control over, and can exchange roles in, their mutual discourse..." (Williams, Rice, and Rogers, 1988, p.10). Others, such as Tannenbaum (1998), define interactivity as the "process of engagement between two communicators in which each causes change and reactions in the other."

Interaction between Learner and Other Learners

In the traditional classroom environment, group interaction (discussions, problem solving, and brainstorming) occurs in a face-to-face mode. The group communication experience can produce, when properly executed, a positive outcome resulting from the intellectual synergy that an individual experiences from sharing ideas and developing concepts in a nonlinear way. It can also expose learners to other cultures and enhance their learning experience by allowing them to benefit from the strengths of each other.

While learners may engage in cognitive analysis individually in an effective way, the achievement of cognitive objectives requiring synthesis and evaluation may be enhanced through interaction between learners. Synthesis requires rearranging elements that were decomposed in analysis. When learners each bring their analytical perspectives into the classroom and share their multiple perspectives in a group interactive session, the group environment can help facilitate the creation of new patterns of understanding built on the foundation of shared individual perspectives. These multiple perspectives also facilitate the process of evaluation of concepts, as learners begin to assign relative value to the individual perspectives.

Interaction between learners is seen as an essential element in the learning process by some theories (especially cooperative learning and to some degree the constructivist models). As such, designers of DL courses must seriously consider whether there is a need for media that enable communication between learners and in which form (synchronicity of communication will be discussed in the next section). In a recent evaluation of 23 cyber courses at a United States academic institution students highlighted the lack of student-student interaction as a major problem (Taylor and Burnkrant, 1998). Some of the findings indicate that a majority of students felt more isolated from others, worked less on assignments with others, and were less likely to ask and receive comments from other students on their own work.

Interaction between Content and Learner

Instructional systems designers use the term interactivity to describe the degree of intellectual, emotional, and physical engagement of the learner to the instructional content using computer-based distance learning technologies. Included in this concept of interactivity are various ways the instructional content is designed for navigation, searches, decision trees, and branching operations. Each of these is discussed in a separate subsection below.

Navigation through the Instructional Content

The technologies presented in chapter three use one of three ways of presenting the material to the learner: hierarchical, sequential, and hypertext (McCormack and Jones, 1997). In a hierarchical environment, the material is presented such that the learner sees information at a certain level and can then drill down to a more detailed level of information for each particular topic. In a sequential learning environment, the learner sees page after page (pages being broadly defined here) of information in a sequential format like reading a book, viewing a video, or seeing a graphical presentation. Traditional textbooks require and are limited to a sequential and linear progression through text and graphics, referred to as "page turning". Finally, hypertext uses pages that are interlinked with one another to allow learners to control the sequence of the material that is presented. While there are risks that learners can get "lost" in hypertext environments, they have gained substantial acceptance as user interfaces to wealth of information with the Web. Hypertext is also becoming popular in the design of distance education and training courses for other non Web-based instructional technologies such as computer-based training. These presentation structures can be combined to provide the best environments possible for learning to occur. Because the use of hypermedia is becoming so popular for several of the instructional technologies described in the next chapter, its advantages and disadvantages are discussed below.

Hypermedia. Some of the instructional technologies that use hypermedia as an interface between the learner and the instructional content include computer-based training, computer-aided instruction, and Web-based training. Some of the material used in teleconferencing sessions can even be organized using hyperlinks. The original work on hypertext was done in the mid-1960s, but it really took off, as an interface, after it had become the Web's way of presenting material in the early 1990s.

Hypermedia Characteristics. The distinguishing feature of hypermedia is that several documents can be linked to one another. Hypertext documents are text files that are formatted using a markup language. Hypermedia can be defined as non-sequential writing where multiple types of data can be incorporated into files (e.g., text, images, graphics, videos, animated images, audio, and virtual reality environments). A document can be linked to specific sections of another document, which can then be linked back to the main document, or linked to any other documents. By simply clicking on the "link", users navigate through this sea of documents rather easily. Because hypertext allows documents to be inter-linked, certain course materials that are generic become reusable in multiple courses. The document containing this reusable information (or module) is stored only once on the server, and all documents (courses) that need to reference it simply link to it.

Hypermedia Advantages and Disadvantages. The benefits to hypertext include having short documents and having access to worldwide information. Some of the benefits also deal directly with the impacts on learning that hypertext can have, such as integration of multiple modes of learning and learner exploration. It is easy when using hypertext links to incorporate multiple data types or media (images, graphics, text, video clips, audio clips, and animated images) in the course material. Using different media promotes the use of multiple stimuli for learners to absorb the material. Hypermedia is also designed to encourage exploration of the content of a course. As discussed later in this chapter, this increases learner centeredness. Hypermedia enables learners to access instructional content laterally, randomly, vertically, linearly, and in a structured manner.

Conversely, there is a debate whether hypermedia is really better for learning than other interfaces because the knowledge is often organized in a fragmented fashion. Some argue that hypermedia may confuse the novice learners more than help them understand when they see only fragments of information at a time. They may not be able to grasp the overall purpose of each fragment of information received in understanding the global course topic. Fragmentation can be solved by creating maps or guided tours of course Web sites, which would also apply to computer-based training sites (Bateman and Simpson, 1995).

Searching Instructional Content

Web-based and computer-based instruction allow the learner to locate words, phrases, or topics using computerized search programs.

In the traditional learning environment, learners can locate topics using the index or table of contents, but thorough searches are limited to the learner's ability to skim large portions of text rapidly or through the use of short-term memory of contents already read.

Search engine capabilities designed into course material or accessed via course material provide additional learning potential for students or trainees. Use of search engines requires the use of research and learning activities, which are separated in traditional learning environments. Learners experiment with various keywords and combinations intuitively to find the ideal combinations of keywords to use to obtain more precise and targeted results. Frequent "net surfers", for example, become "experts" at using Web-based search engines.

Decision Trees and Branching Operations through Instructional Content

An interactive story has multiple beginnings, middles, and endings. Instructional content can be designed in a similar fashion to have multiple branches or ways to navigate through the instructional content to achieve a learning objective. The more choices that have to be made by learners as they navigate through the instructional content, the greater the level of interactivity between the learners and the content. Designing this material requires a balance between too much branching and too little. If learners are left with very few decisions, the material offers limited interactivity and will not achieve its objective. However, too much interactive content in the form of decision trees or branching operations may confuse rather than help learners.

SYNCHRONICITY

Synchronicity refers to the timing of interaction/communication by persons engaged in the learning experience — learner, instructor, and other participants. Face-to-face interaction is by nature synchronous, e.g., parties in the interaction can both send and receive visual and audio communication simultaneously. This allows for one important component of the learning process: feedback. Learners learn concepts more effectively through trial and error, experimentation, and through interchange of ideas with instructors and other learners. Synchronicity in distance and distributed learning is accomplished through computer-mediated communication (CMC) tools, which allow various degrees of geographic and temporal independence. Distance learning instructional technologies, in turn, vary in the types and quantities of CMC tools they use, and therefore in their ability to accommodate real-time interaction.

Synchronous Learning

Synchronous learning takes place when the learner can interact with the instructor and/or other learners in real time. Communication media vary in their ability to handle real-time communication through audio, video, graphics, and text. In addition to real-time communication, some technologies allow for real-time interactive collaboration — e.g., electronic whiteboards, shared mouse control in applications, and group decision support applications. The value of synchronous learning is that feedback from others in the learning environment (instructor and other learners) is immediate and simultaneous. Feedback is an essential aspect of group learning, collaboration, and problem solving. Some of the distance and distributed learning tools that support synchronous communication and learning include teleconferencing, Web-based teaching with "chat" or multi-user domain (MUD) sessions, and video tele-training.

Asynchronous Learning

Videotapes, CBT, and some Web-based training (WBT) take place asynchronously, i.e., the learner is not in real-time communication with the instructor or with other learners. Some of the Computer-

Figure 2.2 Synchronous Learning

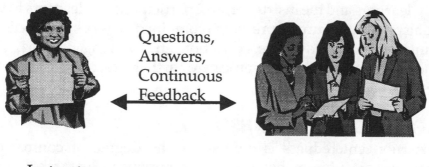

Questions,
Answers,
Continuous
Feedback

Instructor   Learners

Figure 2.3 Asynchronous Learning

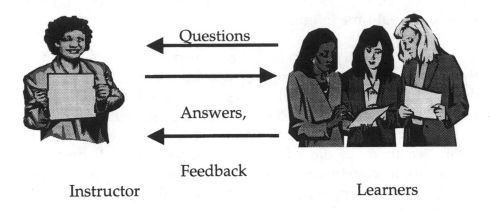

Questions

Answers,

Feedback

Instructor   Learners

Mediated Communication (CMC) technologies that can be used to communicate with the instructor or other learners asynchronously include electronic mail, fax, bulletin boards, and threaded discussions. One of the main advantages of using asynchronous training is that the user controls the pace of the learning process. Learners control both rhythm and rate of their responses and the pace at which they assimilate the material. For example, they are not at a disadvantage because of poor typing skills, which is an issue with some synchronous computer-mediated communication technologies.

Combining Interactivity and Synchronicity

Asynchronous and synchronous learning technologies have varying levels of effectiveness in their ability to support interactivity among learners and the instructor, and participation of learners in the learning process. Figure 2.4 presents a combined view of synchronicity and interactivity in distance education and training courses. The technologies provided as examples are further described in chapter three.

LEARNER CENTEREDNESS

Learner-centeredness is defined as the degree of control the learner has over his or her learning experience. Researchers and educators suggest that the extent to which learner centeredness is implemented will affect the degree of success of an education of

Figure 2.4 Interactivity and Synchronicity in Distance Learning

Synchronicity

		Asynchronous	Synchronous
Level of Interactivity	**Passive**	Learners receive information. They take course at their preferred time. Ex.: non-interactive Computer Based Training (CBT)	Learners receive information. Course is scheduled. Ex.: downlinked videoconferencing course without communication capabilities.
	Participation	Learners make responses to simple instructional cues. They take course at their preferred time. Ex.: interactive CBT	Learners make responses to simple instructional cues. Course is scheduled. Ex.: video teletraining course with student audio participation.
	Real-Time Participation		Learners involved in life-like set of complex cues and responses. Course is scheduled. Ex.: desktop videoconferencing course.

training course (Race and Brown, 1995). Race and Brown argue that learner centric courses that are successful implement four key strategies:

1. Encourage the learner to want to learn.
2. Promote learning by doing (with hands-on practice for example).
3. Provide mechanisms to receive feedback from others.
4. Allow learners to digest the information.

At least three learning theories support the concept that the learner should take control of the learning environment: Cognitive Information Processing, Constructivism, and Socioculturalism models of learning. The theories differ on other dimensions such as what is knowledge and learning, and what level of reality the context of learning promotes (Leidner and Jarvenpaa, 1995). One of their key common elements is that learners differ in their learning style and preferences, and must therefore have control of the pace at which instruction is provided in order to achieve learning in the most effective way.

In distance and distributed learning environments, the simple fact of using computers or some other technology may help promote interest in learning for various individuals (strategy one). Properly designed DL courses should also allow for practical tools and exercises so that the medium used can encourage the learner to "do" instead of just to read (strategy two). This is accomplished by forcing some interactivity between the learner and the instructional content. Similarly, some DL environments are designed to promote rapid and effective feedback (strategy three). This can be implemented via some form of human communication, asynchronous or synchronous, or again via technology trial and error capabilities (interaction between the learner and the technology). For example, computer-based training does not typically offer feedback from other learners, although some feedback can be designed into the material.

COURSE MEDIATION

There are two types of mediation that can be introduced in distance education or training courses: technology and instructor mediation.

Instructor Mediation

The literature in the fields of training and education covers extensively the role of instructors, teachers and tutors in delivering or facilitating learning. It is beyond the scope of this book to provide an extensive discussion of the advantages and disadvantages of instructor-led versus non instructor-led courses. It is important, however, to discuss the role of the instructor with respect to the other learning variables discussed in this chapter and the instructional technologies presented in chapter three.

In the traditional learning environment, instructors transmit instructional content via oral presentation or lectures. In distance and distributed learning environments, instructors may also prepare the material but are able to use technologies for delivery to the learners. In some cases, instructors are not involved in any real-time course delivery, such as computer-based training, videotapes, and some forms of Web-based training. Another important role of instructors, previously described in this chapter, is to interact with learners. One of the most important reasons for interaction is to exchange informa-

Figure 2.5 Instructor Involvement in Distance Learning Instructional Technologies

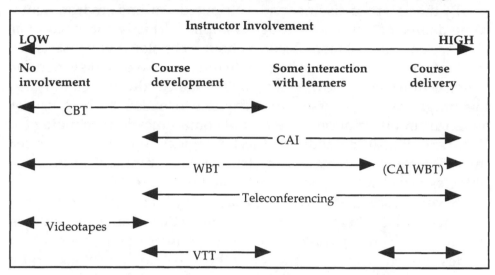

Legend:
CBT   Computer Based Training
CAI   Computer Assisted Instruction
WBT   Web Based Training
VTT   Video Tele-training

tion (including evaluation of learners), but interaction is also useful for providing explanations of complex concepts and to provide learners with a human touch in their courses. Figure 2.5 shows the levels of involvement of instructors in instructional technologies presented in chapter three.

For institutions and organizations contemplating implementation of distance education or training courses, decisions concerning the appropriate level of instructor involvement are important because they have implications for financial and learning outcomes. Instructor time can be expensive, especially if they have to be trained for distributed learning or if they have to travel. Conversely, technology costs for those technologies that partially or totally replace instructors are rapidly decreasing. Therefore, when making a decision as to type of DL environment to provide, organizations must decide the importance that will be placed on learning, learners' satisfaction with their learning environment, and the level of technology costs they are willing to incur.

Technology Mediation

By the nature of distance and distributed learning environments, some degree of technology usage is implied. This is not to say that distance education cannot occur without technology; one just has to think of correspondence courses delivered via the postal system for over a century now. However, today's distance education and training programs and courses are designed to make the best use of advances in information systems and communication technologies. The instructional methods (and technologies) described in chapter three use existing information systems and telecommunication technologies to various degrees, as presented in Figure 2.6.

Several researchers have asked, and tried to answer the question: does technology help learners perform better? Some individuals argue that technology allows the learner to use more senses and modes of learning than instruction without technology. Others argue that technology distracts the learner from the actual content that has to be learned. Several studies have been conducted comparing technology-based and non technology-based education. In a review of a large number of these studies, Russell (1996) reveals that there is no

Figure 2.6 Technology Support for Distance Learning Instructional Technologies

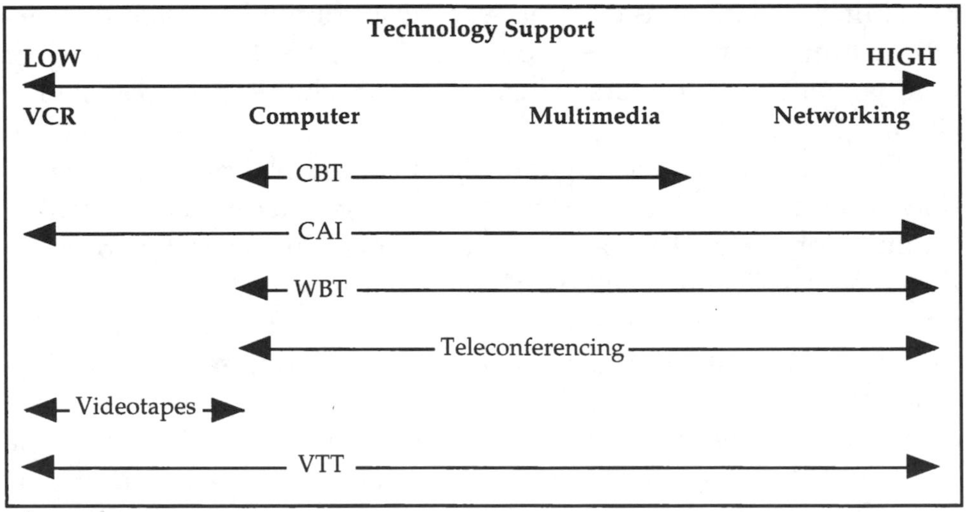

Legend:
CBT   Computer Based Training
CAI   Computer Assisted Instruction
WBT   Web Based Training
VTT   Video Tele-training

significant difference between learning in traditional courses and learning using some form of electronic courses. Others conducting individual studies also found that learning of procedural knowledge does not differ between technology-mediated distance learning courses and traditional courses (Webster and Hackley, 1997). One issue to consider, however, is that learning performance is not the only outcome of importance. Other outcomes such as participation, satisfaction with the learning environment, or costs must also be considered. Other factors to keep in mind with technology usage in distance learning environments include the reliability of the technology itself and the quality of delivery (e.g. audio and video signals). For example, in videoconferencing sessions for distance education, students and instructors highlighted the poor quality of audio and video signals as problems to improve in future courses (Webster and Hackley, 1997).

REUSABLE LEARNING OBJECTS

Most of the learning variables discussed in this chapter deal with learning, often from the learners' point of view. There are other variables that have to be analyzed and evaluated before organizations implement distance learning. One of these is the emerging practice of identifying redundant content among multiple courses, which can then be developed as reusable learning objects. The idea behind reusing learning objects is that part of the material that is used in one course can be reused in other courses as well. Some technologies like computer-based training and Web-based training are particularly suitable for implementing repositories of reusable learning objects. For example, in Web-based training, modules can be created and stored in one place but be linked to multiple courses via hyperlinks.

Reusable Learning Objects have several advantages:

1. The content can be designed into modules. These are more focused and can be developed by experts.
2. Reusing existing high quality material substantially saves on instructor time.
3. Using learning objects, different courses that share the same basic content will be consistent in knowledge delivery to the learners.

SUMMARY OF LEARNING VARIABLES

While DL instructional technologies will be presented more at length in chapter three, it is useful to summarize how each of them meets or supports certain learning variables that have been presented in this chapter. Table 2.1 shows a matrix of each of the learning variables and the instructional technologies. A mark in the table indicates that the technology meets or supports the learning variable, even if only to a limited degree. Further explanations regarding the technologies and what they do and do not support will be provided in the next chapter.

Table 2.1 Summary of Learning Variables Support by Instructional Technologies

Learning Variables	CBT	CAI	WBT	TC	VT	VTT
Learning Objectives						
Cognitive	√	√	√	√	√	√
Psycho-motor	√	√	√			
Affective		√	√	√		√
Interaction						
Learner-Instructor		√	√	√		√
Learner-Learner		√	√	√		√
Learner-Content	√	√	√			
Synchronicity						
Asynchronous	√	√	√		√	
Synchronous		√	√	√		√
Learner-Centeredness	√		√			
Course Mediation						
Instructor-led		√	√	√		√
Technology-mediated	√	√	√	√	√	√
Reusable Learning Objects	√	√	√			

Legend: CBT: Computer-Based Training, CAI: Computer-Assisted Instruction, WBT: Web-Based Training, TC: TeleConferencing, VT: Videotape, VTT: Video Tele-Training

Chapter III

Distance Learning Technologies

There are many technologies that can be used to support distance education and training. Some are used as supplements to traditional classroom environments; others are used as complete replacements for traditional lecture-based courses. While each technology might be better suited for one type of environment than another, it is important to consider its relative advantages and disadvantages. For example, some of them provide almost no interaction or communication between the learner and the instructor, or between learners. Some technologies provide limited contextual information besides the lecture material, while others provide the interested learner with a wealth of additional information. Consistent with chapter two, we must also note that some technologies allow for more flexibility by providing asynchronous support for learning, allowing learners to work at their own pace, while others are limited to a synchronous learning environment that also provides more communication possibilities. This chapter presents an overview of the various technologies that are being used in distance and distributed learning.

What is meant exactly by technology? The term includes those tools that provide access to education or training, such as telecommunication networks, computers, or books. These are referred to as delivery technologies (Clark, 1994). There are also tools that influence the learning experience of learners such as tests, tutorials, exercises, help guides or examples and these are referred to as instructional technologies (Clark, 1994) or teaching strategies (also including lectures, group and individual projects, drills and experiential work). The term instructional technology used in this chapter encompasses all combinations of tools to deliver and enhance learning. The ideal technology for an organization depends on the particular course, the audience, the financial means of the organization, and its existing technology infrastructure. Table 3.1 presents an overview of the advantages and disadvantages of the DL technologies presented in this chapter.

COMPUTER-BASED TRAINING

Computer-based training has regained popularity in organizations in recent years. Other terms often used to refer to a similar set of tools include computer-based tutorials and computer-based teaching. Computer-based training involves training courses that are offered on a computer, typically distributed on CD-ROM or diskettes. An ideal situation is to offer the course on CD-ROM while allowing the users access to the hard drive to save data for actual hands-on practice. CBTs can be used as media for tutorials or complete lectures. Learners using CBT courses are able to study the material for the given course at their own pace. Many corporations are equipped with learning labs. A typical learning lab is configured with computers on desks separated by dividers, and a library of courses. As employees require training, they can reserve space in the room and sign up for the particular course of interest to them. Often, these CBT courses can be used as preparation or follow up to more traditional classroom workshops.

In the past, CBT courses were accompanied by textbooks, whereas today most of these courses are supplemented with on-line material. In recent years, CBT courses have increasingly been developed for multimedia delivery. Interactive multimedia instructions allow learners to read text, view (images or videos), and hear information, while they practice their knowledge on interactive exercises using the computer. Interactive multimedia courses can be developed with a number of commercially available tools and software packages. Tools

Table 3.1 Advantages and Disadvantages of Instructional Technologies

Instructional Technology	Advantages	Disadvantages
Computer-Based Training (CBT) - Instruction delivered on a computer without instructor involvement.	• Temporal independence (L) • Increased learner centeredness (L) • Modularity (L) • Immediate feedback (L) • Rapid response time (L) • Scheduling flexibility (O) • Operational costs (O)	• Lack of interaction (L) • Lack of instructor (L) • No control of learning environment (L) • Access to computer required (L) • Platform dependence (O) • Implementation costs (O) • Costly revisions (O) • No control of results (O)
Videotapes - Instruction delivered on videotapes that can viewed asynchronously.	• Temporal independence (L & I) • Geographic independence (L) • Limited requirements (L) • Scheduling flexibility (O) • Overall costs low (O)	• No feedback (L) • One mode of learning only (L) • Lack of interaction (L) • Lack of instructor (L) • No control of learning environment (L) • Difficult revisions (O) • No control of results (O) • Security (O)
Computer Aided Instruction (CAI) Web-based or computer-based tools to assist regular instruction.	• Improved learning (L and O) • Increased learner centeredness (L) • Scheduling flexibility (learner) • Modularity (L) • Immediate feedback (L) • Multiple modes of learning used (L) • Teaching flexibility (I) • Individual attention to learners (I) • Operational costs (O) • Course standardization (O) • Development costs (O)	• Limited interaction between learners (L) • Increased coordination (I) • Platform dependence (O) • Development costs (O)
Web-Based Training (WBT) - Instruction delivered via a computer connected to a network (Internet/Intranet).	• Free software (L) • Geographic independence (L & O) • Temporal independence (L & O) • Increased learner centeredness (L) • Ease of use (L & I) • Increased interaction with instructor (L) • Increased interaction with other learners (L & I) • Inexpensive communication tools (L & I) • Up-to-date courses (L) • Everything is digital (I) • Platform independence (I & O) • Link to extra resources (I) • Reusability (I) • Future growth (I & O) • Use of existing infrastructure (O) • Centralized result tracking (O)	• Reliance on ISP (L, I & O) • Low speed connections (L) • Viruses (L & I) • Computer access required (L) • Network access costs (L) • Quality of material (L) • Security and privacy (L, I & O) • Increased overall costs (L) • "Lost on the web" (L) • Reliance on electronic communication (L & I) • Increased coordination (I) • Digital material required (I) • HTML knowledge required (I) • Dependence on course builder (I) • Copyright issues (I) • Authentication (I) • High speed connections required (O) • Instructor training required (O) • Lack of standards (O) • Support infrastructure (O) • Implementation and overall costs (O)

Table 3.1 (continued) Advantages and Disadvantages of Instructional Technologies

Instructional Technology	Advantages	Disadvantages
Teleconferencing Applications - Instruction delivered via data, audio or video conferencing tools. Synchronous.	• Face-to-face (L & I) • Learner-learner interaction (L) • Learner-instructor interaction (L & I) • Geographic independence (L & O) • Complex problems explained (L & O) • Ease of revision (O) • Operational costs – desktop (I)	• Bandwidth requirements (L & I) • Audio limitations (L & I) • Video limitations (L & I) • No off-line work (L) • Implementation costs (O) • Security and privacy (O)
Video Tele-Training (VTT) - Instruction delivered using live video (one or two way) and two-way audio.	• Real-time capabilities (L) • Up-to-date courses (L) • Learner-learner interaction (L) • Learner-instructor interaction (L) • Dynamic updates (I) • Interaction with learners (I) • Geographic reach (O) • Operational costs (O) • Reusability of infrastructure (O)	• Scheduling (L & I) • Geographic dependence (L) • Visual display limitations (L) • Increased coordination (I) • Difficult participation of learners (I) • Dependence on support personnel (I) • Training required (O) • Implementation costs (O) • Production personnel required (O)

Legend: L = advantage to learners; I = advantage to instructors; O = advantage to organizations

for courseware development are addressed in chapter five.

There is a vast inventory of CBT courses available commercially. Some types of courses, such as computer programming, are particularly suitable for CD-ROM media. For example, a program called Learnfortran is used in schools to teach both programming principles and the FORTRAN language (Bateman and Simpson, 1995). Another example is mathematics where several institutions have developed or bought math courses for their freshman students (e.g., MathWise in Britain or the Math Emporium at Virginia Polytechnic Institute and State University in the United States).

Requirements and Design

One of the issues with several CBT courses is the customization required to meet the particular needs of an organization. While the cost of acquiring a course on CD-ROM may be reasonable, the cost of creating a new course on CD-ROM can be very high. The most expensive component of courseware development is that of personnel labor, not hardware and software. The degree to which a course is well-designed is directly related to the effectiveness of course delivery

(Stanton and Stammers, 1990). Therefore organizations should pay careful attention to courseware design. The most important design considerations to focus on are summarized below.

Multimedia Capabilities

Designers should take advantage of the multimedia capabilities of CBT software development tools to include static media (text, graphics and images) integrated with dynamic media (audio, video and animation).

Common and Consistent Interface

The CBT should be easy to use and intuitive in design. One of the main advantages of today's graphical user interfaces is the ability to represent graphically complex structures. An effective graphical user interface includes well-designed icons and navigation aids with a systematic and clear organization (Scotney and McClean, 1995), help tools, explanatory error messages, and a limited amount of information at a time on the screen (Race and Brown, 1995). Error messages are an integral and important part of the learning process, where individuals can learn from the mistakes they make in using a particular software or testing their knowledge of a particular topic (Race and Brown, 1995). Buttons should be designed for clarity and should be used consistently. For example, if the "Return to Main Menu" button on one screen is on the top right corner, it should be located at the same place on every screen. There should be easy to follow and understand navigation tools to make it simple for the learner to find his or her way back to the main thread of the course.

Organization of Documents

Early versions of CBT software used a menu-based approach within a hierarchical structure. Today, hyperlinks are used more frequently as CBT interfaces. Given the similarity between hyperlinked Web pages and hyperlinked course software, users tend to be familiar with the idea of clicking on a word or sentence to get further information on a particular topic. In CBT courses hyperlinks are often used to provide definitions, for example on CD-ROM encyclopedias like Encarta (Registered trademark of Microsoft Corporation). Some tools for developing on-line course material are specifically designed to create hyperlink-liked documents. Hypertext CBTs have been found useful by most learners (Scotney and McClean, 1995). The best way to have a valid organization for these courses is to use the storyboard as a planning tool. The storyboard lays out the complete set of pages to be used before any of the actual development starts.

Content of CBTs

Because CBTs are used in self-paced delivery, it is important to provide the learner with as many tools for learning as possible. It has been shown that the more senses used in the learning process, the greater the rate of retention and the more rapid the recall of the material (Gardner, 1993). CBTs offer that possibility beyond what can be offered in a traditional lecture environment. Videos, audio, images, text, hypertext, and animation can all be combined to provide the most complete environment possible for learning. The level of vocabulary used should be consistent with the intended audience. Finally, since CBT courses do not require a connection to a network, and since powerful personal computers are affordable, CBTs can be designed with high quality graphics that will capture the attention of the learner.

Interactivity

An important consideration for CBT courses is the interactivity they provide between the material and the learner. It is not sufficient anymore to provide courses that are "page turners" – material read sequentially by the learner. To achieve learning effectiveness, course designers must force the learners to perform some actions as well (Race and Brown, 1995). One of the key aspects of interactivity that makes training more personal is the ability to make the learner part of the learning system. Interaction with the instructional content makes the training more personal. An example is when learners are asked to enter their first name as they start the course or tutorial, which is then used by the system when providing feedback to the learner (Race and Brown, 1995). Race and Brown suggest that feedback should be provided on both "good answers" and "bad answers." Learners should also be allowed to perform some work on disks that they can take back with them to practice the material learned in training.

In order to plan, create, and implement CBT courses, the following may be required:

- Multimedia computers with medium to high processing power and high memory capacity.
- Multimedia peripherals such as microphones, earphones, video cards, audio cards, high resolution screens), and CD-ROM drives.
- Multimedia development software (if courses are to be built in-house) such as Adobe Premiere®, Adobe PhotoShop®, various QuickTime tools, etc.
- Quiet (office or home) learning environment for the learner to take these courses.
- CD burners (if courses are developed by the organization).
- Action recorder software. These software programs allow the course designer to record series of actions on the computer screens. Examples include Lotus ScreenCam® (http://www.lotus.com/home.nsf/welcome/screencam/) or Microsoft's DirectShow® (http://www.microsoft.com/directx/overview/dshow/).

Advantages

Learner
1. *Temporal Independence.* Learners can work at their own pace and convenience.
2. *Increased Learner-Centeredness.* Learners have more control over their learning environment and can work at their own pace on some of the material. Using audio, video, animations and other interactions increase the learner's interest .
3. *Modularity.* Designing modular courses is easy in a CBT environment. Learners can take classes in modules instead of complete courses.
4. *Immediate Feedback.* Learners taking these courses can use the built-in tutorials and quizzes to obtain immediate feedback on their performance on the given topic under study.
5. *Multiple Modes of Learning.* The learners use multiple modes of learning through a variety of stimuli (audio, video, text) built into the course environment.
6. *Rapid Response Time.* Access to information on CD-ROM is very efficient, especially when compared to access to remote computer systems using communication facilities or the Internet. This

allows the designers to incorporate better quality graphics, and in larger quantities, into the course material.

Institution

1. *Temporal Independence.* Since there are no instructors required for CBTcourses, the course can be developed by an independent team of instructors at a time convenient to the organization.
2. *Scheduling Flexibility.* For courses that are taken sporadically by a large number of employees, CBT courses help avoid scheduling issues and having many employees off "productive" time at the same time.
3. *Cost.* The cost per student of producing courses that are taken by a large number of employees or students repeatedly is low. In addition, compared to instructor-led training, cost savings in the long run could be substantial (including instructor time, instructor training, and travel time).

Disadvantages

Learner

1. *Interaction Between Learners.* Since all learners take the course at a convenient time for themselves, there is no interaction between learners. Interaction has been shown to help substantially in the learning process.
2. *Lack of Instructor.* There is no instructor available to help with difficult concepts or to guide the learner in the learning process.
3. *Control of Learning Environment.* Institutions have no control over the learning environment in which the student or trainee takes a CBT course. Some home environments, for example, may be inappropriate for learning because the learner must manage child care or other duties while trying to learn, or because there is no quiet space available for the learner.
4. *Computer Access.* Most organizations provide some office or room for employees wishing to take CBT courses. Conversely, when individuals want to take courses on their own, for personal reasons or as part of a continuing education program, they must have access to the minimum computer configuration required for playback of the CD-ROM course, which includes a multimedia

capable personal computer.

Institution

1. *Platform Dependence.* The institution must create several sets of the same material if it uses multiple platforms within its environment (for example, Unix vs. Windows, or Macintosh vs. IBM compatible personal computers).
2. *Development Costs.* If there are no generic courses available for the organization's purposes, substantial costs are involved in the design and development of customized course material. This can only be financially justified if there is a large number of learners who will enroll in the course.
3. *Ease of Revisions.* Any needed update to the content of a course requires substantial efforts and costs to modify the material and re-burn a set of compact disks. The "outdated" disks often have to be discarded.
4. *Control of Results.* Unless the institution decides to use testing tools after individuals have taken a particular CBT course, there is no assessment of these individuals' learning.

Summary

In summary, CBT tools are amenable to the design of several kinds of courses. They can use presentation styles that go from lecture type material to simulation and visualization tools. With the ever-decreasing costs of memory, processing power, and other hardware; and with advances in software and hardware multimedia tools, CBT courses are regaining the popularity they once had in corporations. They represent good alternatives for distance training in situations where learners can study at their own pace, individually, and where the organization has enough potential learners to justify the cost of development.

Table 3.2 Summary of Requirements and Target for CBT Courses

Requirements			Target
Hardware	**Software**	**Other**	**Target**
• Multimedia computers • Multimedia peripherals • CD-ROM burners	• Multimedia development software • Action recorder software	• Course developer or development support personnel • Quiet learning space	**Total conversion or combined delivery** • Self-motivated learners • Large number of potential learners

COMPUTER-AIDED INSTRUCTION

Description

Several terms are used to refer to the same basic instructional technology approach: Computer-aided learning (CAL), computer-based learning (CBL), computer-based teaching, computer-aided teaching, or compute-aided instruction (CAI). CAI is similar to CBT but is typically used as an add-on or complement to traditional learning methods. These instructional technologies are often used to provide tutorials delivered in computer laboratories to supplement lecture-based instruction and to provide hands-on exercises to learners. In order to provide greater efficiency in teaching, these technologies are often implemented and used as complements to classroom work.

For the past few decades, CAI tools took one of two forms: specially designed software programs focusing on specific topics (for example learning foreign languages on CD-ROM), or generic software used to perform exercises created and given by the instructors (for example using Microsoft's Excel® to practice accounting problems). These were performed on computers either at home or in computer laboratories. Recently, the Internet has started playing an increasing role in CAI by providing "on-line" tools on the Web to complement classroom instruction. CAI on the Web is now being used by many university professors for educational purposes. Originally, most of them used the Web solely as a delivery mechanism for information, but today more of them use it to provide additional exercises or communication facilities for students. Web-based training will be covered in the following section, but it must be remembered that a lot of what is discussed there also applies to CAI.

Requirements and Design

The design of CAI courses is very similar to that of CBT. The main difference is that CBT material must be inclusive of all information since the learner cannot obtain clarifications from instructors. In CAI, instructors are typically able to provide substantial information to learners in regular classroom sessions or via telecommunication facilities. As such, the design of modules or tutorials may require less complete sets of information and does not require the inclusion of communication facilities. Some of the tools that can be used for CAI include tutorials, simulations, help guides, or reference information. Some of the design issues discussed here are similar to those found in the CBT section.

Multimedia Capabilities

Designers should take advantage of the multimedia capabilities of CAI software development tools to include static media (text, graphics and images) integrated with dynamic media (audio, video and animation). This allows learners to use multiple modes of learning through varied stimuli.

Interface

The CAI software should be easy to use and self-explanatory (good icons, navigation tools, systematic and clear organization, help tools, clear error messages, and limited amount of information at a time).

Organization of Documents

Starting with a storyboard to plan the course or tutorial content, the documents should be organized in an easy to find/follow nature for the learner, using either hierarchical or hypertext presentation structures.

Interactivity

Just as it is important in CBT courses, interactivity between the material and the learner should be included in CAI courses or tutorials. This includes providing frequent and useful feedback, which should be provided for both "good answers" and "bad answers" as these both play important roles in learning. Interactivity is again facilitated by allowing learners to do some of their course work on disk (a:\ drive) so that they can keep their practice work after they leave the course environment, while retaining the integrity of the material on CD-ROMs by making it read-only.

Topic Specific

Courses for CAI have to be tailored to the particular topic that is being taught. As they are usually used as complements to classroom lectures, they should be closely related to that particular material. The ideal CAI tools allow the learner the possibility of applying the concepts previously learned. In these situations, courses or tutorials must be developed in-house, the same way CBT courses have to. This does not preclude the use of generic software packages when appropriate.

Hardware, software and other requirements for creating and implementing CAI courses include:

- Multimedia computers with medium to high processing power and large memory capacity.
- Multimedia peripherals such as microphones, earphones, video cards, audio cards, high-resolution screen, and CD-ROM drives
- Multimedia development software (if courses are to be built in-house) such as Adobe Premiere®, Adobe PhotoShop®, various QuickTime tools, etc.
- CD burners (if courses are to be built in-house).
- Screen movement capture software (such as ScreenCam® and DirectShow® previously discussed in the CBT section).

Advantages

Learner

1. *Improved Learning.* Computer-assisted teaching has been said to enhance learners' learning capability (Darby, 1992).
2. *Increased Learner Centeredness.* Learners can study tutorials or add-on material at their own pace and at the appropriate time for them. This is particularly important for learners who suffer from not being able to follow the pace of the lectures, but who have the capabilities of catching up and finding the missing information by studying on their own.
3. *Scheduling Flexibility.* Learners often have the flexibility of deciding when they want to take the particular computer modules that are necessary for them to complete their classroom work. This allows them substantial scheduling flexibility.
4. *Modularity of Courses.* Designing a modular course is easy in CAI environments. Modules are useful supplements for lecture material and can be assigned at the appropriate time when the necessary prerequisite material has been covered. For learners, this provides an opportunity to perform some experiential work as required for each topic discussed in class, while not overloading them with information and homework.

5. *Immediate Feedback.* Similar to CBT, learners can use the built-in tutorials and quizzes to obtain immediate feedback on their performance on the topic they are studying.
6. *Using Multiple Modes of Learning.* Similar to CBT, courses can be designed so that learners use multiple modes of learning through a variety of stimuli (audio, video, text) that can be built into the course material and environment.

Instructor

1. *Teaching Flexibility.* Instructors are able to combine lecture material with specific modules offered using CAI tools. This permits instructors to devote more time, if required, to covering concepts in class, while letting students learn the hands-on portion of the course on their own.
2. *Individual Attention to Learners.* Learners work at their own pace on the CAI tools, allowing the instructor to devote more time individually to learners requiring more attention.

Institution

1. *Reduced Operational Costs.* For courses requiring substantial training on the computer by a large number of learners, fewer instructors may be required for teaching or training these large groups. The groups can be taught the lecture portion of the course in large sections, and then be split up to take the tutorials at their own pace individually or in small groups.
2. *Course Standardization.* For courses where there is a large number of potential learners, CAI tools help achieve a certain level of standardization in the quality and quantity of material received by all learners. Typically, when a large number of learners must take a similar course, several instructors are assigned to teach the material. While styles may differ between instructors, the content of the hands-on component is standardized if all learners use the same CAI tool.
3. *Lower Course Development Cost.* By centralizing the development of some of the learning tools, institutions may free up time for instructors to focus on other important teaching or training matters.
4. Improved Learning. In a meta-analytic study of over one hundred evaluations of the use of CBT in courses and programs,

Kulik (1994) found that:
- Students learn more in those classes.
- Students learn lessons in less time.
- Students like their classes more.
- Students develop more positive attitudes towards computers.

Disadvantages

Learner
1. *Limited Interaction Between Learners.* Some interaction exists between learners when they complete the non-CAI part of their course, if they are in a traditional lecture environment. If CAI is combined with other non communication supported distance education or training course (communication support is discussed in the following section on Web-Based Training), then there is no interaction between learners. Such interaction is usually beneficial to most learners involved.

Instructor
1. *Increased Coordination.* Instructors who adopt CAI tools as part of their course face substantial efforts to coordinate the CAI part which is typically offered in special computer laboratories or on Internet connected computers. This coordination is in addition to the traditional material they must prepare and deliver for the course.

Institution
1. *Platform Dependence.* Similar to CBT, the institution must create several sets of the same material if it uses multiple platforms within its environment (for example, Unix vs. Windows, and Macintosh vs. IBM compatible).
2. *Development Costs.* CAI material is often tailored to particular topics, and as such, is most often developed by the institution's employees. There are some general tutorial type software programs available, for example, to teach mathematics or programming languages. When there are no generic courses available, there are substantial costs involved in development of course material. This can only be justified if there is a potential for a large

number of learners to take the course, and if the material is relatively stable over time.

Summary

Computer-aided instruction is most often used as technology insertion in the traditional classroom environment. The CAI is used to complement or supplement traditional teaching or training with hands-on practice, tests, tutorials, help guides or modules that can be accessed on CD-ROM in computer labs (requiring the learner to travel to the lab) or on the Internet. As such, CAI by itself is not a technology sufficient to provide DL. It must be used in combination with other distance delivery tools and can, when used appropriately, significantly enhance individuals' learning experience.

WEB-BASED TRAINING

Description

Web-Based Training (WBT) uses the Internet (or Intranet) as its primary medium for delivery of instruction. Even though it is defined as Web-based, several tools used within this type of instructional technology are non Web-based, such as file transfer protocol (FTP), Usenet, Internet Mail, Telnet, Listservs, or Chat rooms. WBT can take one of two forms; it can be used to supplement regular type courses (as a form of CAI), or it can be used to replace courses that were or would have been offered in regular classrooms. Such courses are then referred to as Web-based courses, cybercourses or virtual courses. In these situations, WBT often allows students to work at their own pace (in cyber courses), emphasizing the learner-centered role of this technology in education and training.

As a CAI tool, WBT is often used solely for information distribution, a function that is particularly well served by hypertext. WBT allows the distribution of course material to take place any time and anywhere around the globe, and it has gained unprecedented popularity in academic circles. The present section focuses on offering education or training completely via Web-based courses. Some of the techniques and tools discussed within this section, however, can be used to supplement and complement regular courses (thereby using the Web for CAI).

A characteristic of WBT courses is that they typically make extensive use of hypermedia. Chapter two described the pros and cons of hypermedia as a presentation structure for learning material. Another major characteristic that differentiates WBT from the other types of distance education and training instructional technologies discussed so far is its ability to offer communication capabilities. WBT allows interactions between learners and between learners and instructors using a variety of communication facilities such as electronic mail, listservs (computer conferencing), and chat facilities. This capability to offer interactivity makes WBT more appropriate than other types of computer technologies for delivery of distance education and training for courses where such communication is of prime importance. For example, courses in communication or journalism, where the computer cannot really evaluate and comment on the writing (or oral presentations) of learners, are particularly appropriate for this DL environment. Evaluations of WBT programs and courses should

Figure 3.1 An Example of a Web-Based Course
(Reproduction with permission by Virginia Tech's Institute of Distance and Distributed Learning)

therefore differentiate between stand-alone Web-based courses and communication supported Web-based courses. A further breakdown of WBT alternatives is provided in the following subsection.

Types of Web-Based Training

Instruction can be delivered both asynchronously and synchronously at different levels of complexity over the Internet. Some of the different types of WBT alternatives (Barron et al, 1999) are presented below.

Asynchronous Correspondence

The Internet can be used for non-browser-based training over the Internet in situations where bandwidth is severely limited. Correspondence training using file transfer or e-mail to deliver course materials, and Listservs or bulletin boards for communication with the instructor or other learners is similar to paper-based correspondence courses, except that materials are transmitted and received over the Internet. The advantages of such delivery is the low demand on bandwidth, the "low tech" approach that is universally available to anyone with access to the Internet. This may be the appropriate way to deliver training to learners that reside in locations with unreliable Internet connectivity, low bandwidth infrastructure, or intermittent connectivity (e.g., aboard a ship). The disadvantage of such a low technology approach to training is similar to paper-based correspondence courses: communication with the instructor is sequential and delayed.

Synchronous Collaboration

Synchronous collaboration over the Internet requires real-time communication among the participants. This can be accomplished using Web "chat" forums, audio-conferencing, video conferencing, shared whiteboards and collaboration software. The advantages of training in an environment of synchronous collaboration is that participants may interact in real time, no special equipment is required for students to participate other than a Web browser, and hands-on experience can be accomplished through shared mouse control of applications.

Web Enhanced Courses

When traditional classroom instruction is combined with Web technology, it is referred to as "technology insertion" or Web enhancement. This is one of the most popular and widely growing segments of higher education today. Every college and university has some degree of Web enhancement, because it is so easy to implement. Instructors can build an entire Web site for their courses by posting their course syllabus, user manuals, tutorials, help guides, on-line exercises, or practice quizzes. As an instructional support mechanism, Web enhancement is the lowest cost, highest payoff use of the Web. The enhancements provided by the Web can be used to prepare learners before class, for remediation in learning and to provide a useful repository of course materials.

Web Managed Courses

Courses that are managed over the Web, also called course managed instruction (CMI) systems, allow for on-line tracking of learners' performance and learner actions in navigating through the instructional material. Web-managed courses are easy to use, offer collaborative capabilities, password security features, and online testing environments. Web-managed courses require instructor support (however, instructor productivity is achieved because one instructor can support more learners than in the traditional classroom environment). This is a new area of Web-based instruction, and one with great potential, which can include electronic commerce aspects such as course registration and payment, course certification, and transfer of grades and transcripts to external organizations.

Web Delivered Courses

In Web-delivered courses, all materials are available through the Web, with tools for real-time collaboration and interactivity. Web-based courses are easy to update and maintain, are available to anyone around the world with Internet access, and offer course management and multimedia capabilities. However, they can be more complex, time-consuming, and expensive to develop.

Hybrid Delivery

Hybrid delivery systems involve partial Web and partial CD-

ROM course delivery. Large files are downloaded and run locally or provided via CD-ROM. Frequently changing material and smaller files are run from the Web. Hybrid delivery provides the best of both CBT and WBT worlds, and minimizes the disadvantages of each. There are more security options possible, and remote resources are accessible via the Web. Hybrid systems also allow developers to control the user interface more effectively than using the Web alone. The disadvantages may be in the area of distribution (more costly to distribute CD-ROMs), and there may be browser dependency problems with hybrid delivery.

Requirements and Design

Web-Based Training: General

The design of WBT material is facilitated today by a wide variety of tools easily available, very often on the Internet itself. A large number of these tools will be presented in chapter five. There are three aspects of requirements that need to be addressed: how to develop Web-based courses technically, what should be provided in the Web-based environment, and what is the actual content of the course. Content is specific to each course, although some topics can take greater advantage of the Internet environment (for example, courses on data communications). Any course topic can have some degree of content that can be Web-based, to a lesser or greater extent (chapter four will discuss screening for courses). Some of the requirements for the Web-based environment to be provided are as follows:

Help System. WBT material should include a good help system. In Windows-based applications, for example, one expects some help topics to be easily accessible from the last button of the scroll down bar. When custom designing a Web course, developers should think about course specific help topics to be created.

Interface. As with any computer-based tools for teaching or training, the interface should be simple and standard. In WBT, the interface should also provide good navigation tools. Browsers have some basic navigational components (back, forward, and go), but the actual course pages should have their own standard buttons for forward and back, as well as buttons for main page, last page, or other navigation that is important to the course (such as course map). These buttons should clearly and graphically state what their purpose is, and should always be located in the same place on all course pages. This makes it easier for novices to find their way around pages. Dead ends (pages that go nowhere) should also be avoided as should pages that startup new browser windows, as they can confuse learners. Overall, the Web pages should be easy to read and understand. Interfaces, static images, videos, or animated images should be used to make the pages attractive and to keep the interest of learners but should also be used sparingly and carefully as the content is still the key to the learning process.

Images. Images are very nice but should be kept small and should only be used when they add value to the information. Text should be included as alternative to images (alt='text' in HTML) for those viewers who have no image capabilities, or who decide to turn them off because they take too long to download.

Structure. The structure of the Web pages around which a course is designed should allow for easy navigation and for growth. A clear structure will also help when site maintenance is necessary. Often, a map of the site may help not only the learner but also the developer in having a global picture and an understanding of a particular course structure. A link to the course map can be provided as a standard navigation button to help learners in the event that they get "lost" in the course.

Sounds. Audio segments on Web pages can provide significant information to learners. They can also reinforce material that is being viewed by the learner, forcing him or her to use another sense and, thereby enhancing the potential for learning. However, sounds can be tricky to include. The implementation is fairly straightforward. Any digitized audio stream can be "linked to" on a page and when clicked on will start the appropriate client audio playing software. The problem is that these audio software programs are often improperly configured on learners' systems, and there is no way for the instructor to know when this problem occurs. Some students may assume that there is no information available if they click on an audio link that doesn't play. This behavior is a learned behavior from having "surfed the net" to many empty pages and dead ends. They may not even doubt that they have a problem with their audio systems. Specific instructions should be provided to learners on what to do should the audio clip not play when they click on it.

McCormack and Jones (1997) propose that there are four ways to design WBT material:

1. *Distribution*. Documents in almost any standard formats can be linked to directly without conversion very easily using HTML tags. The documents are stored on the server in their original format and are delivered as they are. When a learner wishes to see one of them, he or she simply clicks on the link, their browser will then recognize the file extension and open up the appropriate client software if is installed on the learner's computer (such as Microsoft's Word® and Excel®, or Adobe's Acrobat®). The major advantage of this approach is that it requires almost no investment of time in creating Web pages since only a linking tag (A HREF in HTML) is required. The main disadvantage is that learners must have the appropriate client software installed on their computers to be able to open up these files. Alternatively, they may save the file on disk and then find someone with the appropriate client to open it up later.

2. *Conversion*. The idea here is to take existing material such as Microsoft Word® files and run them through HTML converters. Multiple converters are available on the Internet as shareware or freeware, for example the Internet Assistant (for Microsoft products), Latex2html (for LaTeX conversion), or Rtfoweb (for Rich Text Format conversions, to name just a few. Several converters can be found at the WWW Consortium site (http://www.w3.org/Tools/Word_proc_filers.html) or at one of Yahoo's sites (http://dir.yahoo.com/Computers_and_Internet/Software/Internet/World_Wide_Web/HTML_Converters/). Using converters has the advantage of creating HTML documents so that the learner only requires a browser to access the information. However, it also has the disadvantage of not using the capabilities of hypertext and multimedia to improve course design. Some of the converters also generate HTML code that is not clean and may be difficult to "debug" by the instructor.

3. *Value-Added Conversion*. This requires that conversion of files be performed as described in the previous point, but that the instructor or developer also devotes time to taking advantage of the hypertext and multimedia capabilities offered by the Web environment. This will require coding some links to images, resources

and other files. The advantage is that the material becomes organized in a more learner-centered approach (learners will explore the material instead of just read it). The disadvantage is that this approach requires more time investment than the second approach above, and that it still does not use the Web environment to its outmost capabilities.

4. *Creation*. This is the level of course development where greater effort is required. Courses are built specifically to take advantage of all the capabilities of Web-based environments. In this situation, course developers can include communication facilities built-into the course material to allow learner-learner and learner-instructor interactions. Pages then take full advantage of audio, video and graphic capabilities of the Web. Obviously, this is the most difficult, time consuming and costly approach, but it is also the approach that holds the most potential for full use of the Web's capabilities to enhance learners' education or training. There is a huge quantity of Web authoring tools available for free or for a fee on the Internet (you can see Yahoo's list at http:// dir.yahoo.com/Computers_and_Internet/Software/Reviews/ Titles/Internet/Web_Authoring_Tools/HTML_Editors/). Several software packages also help create complete courses, providing structure and easy to use interfaces for instructors to create their own Web-based courses. Some of these, such as Toolbook, WebFuse or CourseInfo, are discussed in chapter five.

Web-Based Training: Communication Facilities

Learners taking WBT courses from a remote location can have access to other learners, instructors or tutors. This is a major benefit of using WBT instead of CBT. In addition, it has been shown that communication between learners enhances their learning experience. Since it is important in DL environments to facilitate such communication, interactivity capabilities should be designed into these courses when feasible. There are various tools used to include communication capabilities in courses, and the reader is probably quite familiar with most of them. Therefore, they will be only briefly described in this section. It should be noted that three of the four communication tools support asynchronous modes of communication, while one of them is for synchronous communications (chat facilities).

Electronic Mail and ListServs. Electronic mail packages have evolved tremendously in recent years to offer integrated office tools, graphical user interfaces, security features, and interoperability. In addition, electronic mail has been around for long enough that virtually all computer users have adopted the technology, making it an easy tool to incorporate into course requirements. Instructors can disseminate their e-mail address to all learners easily, so that when questions about the material arise, answers can be sent electronically. The response time on these answers, however, will depend on how the instructors or tutors assiduously read their electronic mail. This is a common problem with all asynchronous communication technologies. Also, despite great progress in messaging systems, electronic mail platforms are still not totally compatible, and large files or attachments are not always accessible to all users.

Electronic mail can be used to exchange information between members of groups working on assignments or projects. However, it is most often used in one-to-one communication between learners and instructors. One major advantage of electronic mail is that while several software packages exist, many of them are available (in "lighter" versions) as freeware or shareware on the Internet (for example, Eudora Light at http://www.eudora.com/). In addition, electronic mail functions are incorporated in most of today's browsers, allowing the instructor to require only access to a browser for "attending" a particular WBT course, even when electronic mail communication becomes a requirement. When designing WBT material, course developers can include e-mail hyperlinks at the end of tutorials or particularly complex material which would send mail automatically to the instructor or a tutor.

Use of electronic mail has several other advantages. First it is very inexpensive to use, often adding no software requirements than what would otherwise be needed for a distance education or training course. In addition, it allows the instructor to communicate important information in a timely fashion to students instead of at scheduled times or only when updating the course Web site. Some of its disadvantages, however, include the fact that it has been shown to be a "lean" communication medium as compared to face-to-face interactions (Daft and Lengel, 1986). It is also easy for important messages about a course to be lost in the large quantity of electronic mail messages waiting in an instructor's mailbox or even other learners' mailboxes. Finally, if exchange of information between learners is required, it necessitates that all learners know each other's e-mail addresses, in addition to the instructor's. One solution to this is the use of distribution lists and listservs. When listservs are created, all members of the particular class or group get added to a distribution list. Learners wishing to exchange information with their colleagues just have to remember the name of the list.

Computer Conferencing. Computer conferencing, also called usenets, user discussion forums or threaded discussions, is another asynchronous communication tool. Computer conferencing uses a form of electronic mail as the backbone for communication but handles the information transmitted differently. Information sent to the list gets added to the current discussion. It is therefore possible to keep a record of all exchanges of information between the group members. Learners can then read what has been discussed so far before adding their own comments to the discussion. Over time, the instructor can accumulate a very extensive list of questions and answers, and develop a frequently asked questions (FAQ) section to add to their Web-based course material. Conferencing sessions require space on a server, access permissions, and a moderator, usually the instructor or tutor. Since they are quite easy to setup, conferencing capabilities can be added to WBT courses in the design stage without much effort. In addition no additional software or hardware is required to use the computer conferencing facilities. A sample of conferencing systems available free of charge on the Internet (for testing purposes) include CoW (http://calypso.rs.itd.umich.edu/COW/) for UNIX, Dialogue (http://www.magictree.com/) for Windows, or ConferWeb (http://www.caup.washington.edu/software/conferweb/) for MacIntosh, to name a few.

Some of the greatest benefits of using computer conferencing for communication in Web-based courses is that they help keep a record (a log) of all communications and discussions between group members, which can then be referred to when needed. In addition, computer conferencing allows the discussions to take place between several individuals simultaneously. The disadvantages of this mode of communication for WBT courses is that it remains a lean communication medium. The main disadvantage when compared to electronic mail is that computer conferencing requires more administration for setting up and moderating it throughout the course. This administration is typically handled by the instructor or an assistant.

Bulletin Boards. Bulletin boards are asynchronous communication tools that are also uni-directional. Typically, the instructor posts information on the bulletin board, which is then easily accessible from any remote location. In Web-based course design, there is little need for bulletin boards as posting of information can be done more effectively on the course Web site reserved for that purpose. Because bulletin boards are static, uni-directional, and asynchronous, it is believed that most instructors would prefer the use of Web pages for information dissemination.

Web-Based "Chat" Facilities (including Multi-User Domains (MUDs) and Multi-Object Oriented MUDs (MOOs)). The chat facilities described here are for users of Web browsers or MUDs and MOOs environments only. More advanced chat features will be discussed in the section on teleconferencing. Multi-user domains are environments that simulate full virtual worlds and multi-object oriented MUDs are their OO version. These environments have been used extensively for virtual games where users can get computer-generated objects or characters to "play" using text commands. These environments hold promises for some distance education and training courses.

Chat facilities allow several users to communicate using a common screen area. Everyone in the session can write comments to the groups or private comments to selected individuals. Comments sent to the whole group are then displayed on every participant's screen. Instructors can use these sessions to discuss problems or promote some group communication. Learners can also use chat sessions to help each other out on difficult tasks. Since several "chat" utility software products (also known as Internet relay chats (IRCs)) are freely available for download on the Internet, implementing them is cost efficient and simple. Examples of chat communication packages include: FreeChat (http://www.sonic.net/~nbs/unix/www/freechat/) and IChat (http://www.ichat.com/), again to only name a few.

The advantage of using chat sessions is that they allow many-to-many type communication, where the group can communicate among itself and with the instructor. It is also synchronous, so that questions are answered in real time. Finally, once the WBT course infrastructure is available, adding Web-based chat facilities is very inexpensive. Conversely, synchronicity means that time must be scheduled for the meetings to be held, with all participants available at that time.

Another disadvantage is that the medium for communication remains lean, since text is typed. This also puts the learner with poorer typing skills at a disadvantage compared to his cohort. A server and a dedicated IP address is required to host the chat facility on the instructional side. Finally, if chat sessions are held without the instructor's knowledge, there is no control over the quality and accuracy of the information exchanged.

Requirements

There are several design alternatives for WBT courses, as can be seen from the previous discussion. However, several requirements are standard to support these courses.

Hardware: servers, clients, and network
- Servers. Compared with CBT or CAI courses, WBT requires relatively greater access to personal computers as well as greater computing power. High capacity servers are needed to provide the processing and storage required for Web pages. This includes ensuring that sufficient storage is available for all course pages, and that the server has enough processing power to provide an acceptable response time (although most delays will be caused by communication links).
- Client workstations do not require as much processing power as the server does. Web-based instruction requires only the use of a Web browser. More advanced features that require some processing or compilation may make higher end personal computers a necessity. Whatever the power of the personal computer, however, the monitors available should be as high resolution as possible. Unfortunately, when designing Web-based pages or courses, many designers use images that require high resolution such as complex three-dimensional designs or simulated pictures, but the learners may not have access to monitors of the quality required to clearly view these images.
- Network. To be truly Internet based, the organization must provide TCP/IP networking connections. In addition, since most WBT courses require substantial connect time (and often require even more time for download of software or images), the bandwidth of the network must be sufficient to handle high levels of data transfers. This means that substantial investments must be

made in communication media, software, and hardware. For example, modem pools have to be upgraded to high-speed modems to ensure that users who have high-speed modems can get the best connections possible. Backup networks should also be available, as should advanced network management tools.

Software: Web browsers, electronic mail packages, networking software

- While many of the software programs required for client computers are available as shareware or freeware on the Internet, more advanced networking packages and development tools that must be placed on the server can be expensive. The major costs of developing and implementing WBT courses, however, will remain people costs.

Advantages

Learners

1. *Free Software.* Most of the popular Web browsers needed to view WBT courses are available free of charge on the Internet. The only expense learners may have (besides access to a computer) is for other client software programs that may be required to access some material (for example Microsoft Word to access Word files).

2. *Geographic Independence.* Learners who would otherwise not be able to attend a course because it is offered somewhere where they cannot be physically present can now attend. Because the Internet is used as a backbone for communication and course dissemination in WBT, truly *distributed* learning can be achieved.

3. *Temporal Independence.* When individuals decide to take courses on the Web, they can often work at their own pace, and when they feel it is convenient for them to do so.

4. *Increased Learner Centeredness.* Learners have more control of their learning environment and can work at their own pace on some of the material. Because hypertext encourages learners to explore instead of just read material, they are encouraged to participate in their own learning. Learner centeredness is believed to improve the overall learning experience of those involved.

5. *Ease of Use.* Because WBT courses use a browser as the main interface between the learner and the material, these courses tend

to be fairly easy to use (unless advanced communication facilities are used as well). Since Web browsing is very familiar to a large number of users today, instructors can assume that the easy to use graphical interface should not require much training before learners can use it.

6. *Up-to-Date Courses*. Because of the dynamic nature of Web environments, instructors can update course material as required. Changes in society or in the organization can be reflected in the courses, offering learners the most up-to-date course material that can be offered at that given point in time.

In addition, communication supported WBT tools offer the following advantages:

7. *Increased Communication with Instructor*. Individuals taking training or education courses in a Web-based environment that uses communication facilities will have more opportunities to communicate with an instructor or tutor than with other types of DL technologies. The possibility of interaction is not offered, for example, in videotapes, CBT, and some forms of video-teletraining. While Web-based communication is not the same as face-to-face meetings, learners may overcome some obstacles in their learning by contacting the instructor when appropriate.

8. *Increased Communication with Cohort*. Communication between learners has been shown to enhance learners' overall learning experience. WBT courses often allow individuals to communicate, synchronously or asynchronously, with others involved in the same course, to share information or help each other solve problems.

9. *Inexpensive Communication Tools*. Typical communication tools found in WBT environments are inexpensive, easy to use and/or fairly easy to develop. Several packages are available as freeware on the Internet and can be incorporated without any major programming in existing Web pages.

Instructors

1. *Everything is Digital*. Because all the material that learners submit back via the Internet is digitized, it is much easier for the instructor to deal with learners' work, especially when it is time to evaluate their performance. Everyone who has been involved

with grading student essay questions, for example, knows that deciphering handwriting of some of the students is often a mind boggling task.

2. *Platform Independence.* WBT allows the instructor to prepare course material using their usual and preferred platform. Once the course is published on the Web, the material is accessible by all learners independently of their hardware (for example Macintosh or IBM compatible) and software platforms (for example UNIX or Windows although some limitations will be discussed in the disadvantages section below). This would be in contrast for example, to CBT where the material has to be produced separately for the two main personal computer environments (hardware platforms).

3. *Ease of Use.* The easy to use graphical Web interface means that the instructor has to spend less time on usage instructions and, therefore, can spend more time on content.

4. *Dynamic Updates (Immediacy of Revisions).* One of the main advantages of providing learning material on the Web is that the material can be dynamically changed as needed. The content of the course is therefore less at risk of becoming obsolete (unless the course is never maintained).

5. *Additional Information.* Additional information besides the material for the course can easily be included on Web sites without cluttering the screen so that it is not confused with learning material. Substantial reference material can be offered by adding hyperlinks to such material located at other sites.

6. *Reusability.* Instructors designing and implementing courses on the Web can create and organize the material in modules, so that they or other instructors can reuse some of the modules for other courses.

7. *Future Growth.* Instructors wishing to add to a course that is already implemented on the Web can easily do so. Modules can be added when needed, and additional links can be generated easily.

In addition, for communication supported WBT:

8. *Increased Communication with Learners.* Just as learners benefit from having communication capabilities with their instructor, instructors can benefit from having communication channels to

the learners, so that feedback about course content and presentation can be obtained, and learning effectiveness can be assessed.

9. *Inexpensive and Easy to Use Implementation Tools.* As discussed in a previous paragraph, communication tools are readily available on the Internet for download and fairly easy to integrate into existing Web pages.

Institutions

1. *Use Existing Infrastructure.* Organizations are already investing in Internet or Intranet infrastructures for other commercial purposes. WBT can simply take advantage of their existing infrastructure for knowledge transfer and delivery.

2. *Geographic Independence.* WBT technologies allow organizations to increase the market of learners they can reach by including those individuals who would otherwise not be able to attend courses due to geographic constraints. WBT also allows organizations to offer courses to geographically dispersed learners without having to invest in substantial telecommunication infrastructure as would be required for video tele-training (discussed in a later section).

3. *Temporal Independence.* Another new market that organizations can reach with WBT is individuals who would otherwise not be able to attend these courses because of scheduling constraints.

4. *Platform Independence.* Just as instructors find platform independence to be an advantage when designing WBT courses, institutions find that they do not have to worry about providing different types of computer labs for learners if the material is Web-based. For example, there is no need to have only UNIX based stations or Windows based stations if the material is to be accessed via Web browsers.

5. *Centralized Result Tracking.* In contrast to CBT, using WBT courses allows the organization to have some centralized tracking of learners' performance and results.

6. *Future Growth.* It is easy for institutions, once they have implemented some Web-based courses, to grow their portfolio of courses offered via the Internet. Once some courses have been offered, the infrastructure is in place and the development and implementation knowledge is in-house. Given the modularity of

the client/server computing environment, institutions can grow the networking, processing and storage requirements as they grow their WBT course environment.

Disadvantages

Learners

1. *Reliance on Information System Provider.* Learners who must use the Internet for attending a course are dependent on the Internet provider for the performance of the network. In case of problems with a particular provider, certain individuals may find themselves unable to "attend" their course for a while.

2. *Low Speed Connections.* Many individuals who connect from their homes to Web-based courses use fairly low-speed connections (14.4 KBPS to 33.6 KBPS). However, they are also typically required to stay connected for long periods of time. If there are a large number of files to download, or even few files to download but which are quite large, this becomes an issue. Any large graphic will require substantial download time when using a modem, and often this time cannot be used to perform other tasks on the personal computer. Alternatively, instructors could provide the needed software on large capacity (100 Mb) disks, but this would require learners to have these special drives on their computers.

3. *Viruses.* Instructors and learners alike increase the risks of "contracting" a computer virus as they start exchanging files on the Web (or any other electronic means).

4. *Computer Access Required.* The learners must have access to a personal computer that has at least a Web browser installed (in addition to all other minimum software requirements), as well as communication capabilities (including both hardware and software components).

5. *Network Access Costs.* Learners who must access the Internet from their homes must have an Internet access facility. Students in large institutions typically get free or relatively inexpensive access to electronic mail and the Internet. Workers in large corporations can typically use their office computers for WBT or in some cases they can have free access to their company's servers from home. All others must buy a connection with an Internet

Service Provider.

6. *Quality of Material*. One of the biggest problems of Web-based material in general is the lack of control of the quality of the information provided. The same can be said of educational material on the Web, for which there is no uniform quality standards. Erroneous information can often be included on Web pages that look "official". When pages reference other Web-based material, there is no guarantee that the information will be current, or even accurate, as much of the Web information is not "verified" in any way and is created by whoever wants to put up a page.

7. *Security and Privacy*. Since the instructor and learners exchange a large quantity of information on the Internet, and since some of the information placed on the Web is personal, there are several privacy concerns that learners could have (even when some security features are used). For example, grade checkers are often used to display student grades, based on user IDs, social security numbers or passwords. If an individual gets access to the list of passwords, he or she could know the grades of all other learners. Similarly, security is always a concern when information is exchanged on public networks. For example, if a course provides training to employees on some company features that are going to provide competitive advantage in the short term, there is an increased risk of breaches if the information is the subject of a course and is included in the on-line material.

8. *Increased Overall Costs*. Learners who use their own computers to access the WBT courses must acquire fairly high end personal computers that have multimedia capabilities and high resolution monitors. In addition, if learners work from home on these courses, and must therefore stay connected for long periods of time, they will require a second phone connection to their home, adding to their personal costs. Finally, a printer is almost a necessity for working on Web-based courses. Several writers have suggested that by implementing WBT, institutions have actually been successful at shifting some of the costs of providing education or training to the learners.

9. *Learning Environment*. Instructors have no control over the learning environments in which individual learners take a course.

Some home environments, for example, may be inappropriate for learning because individuals must handle child care while trying to learn, or because there is no quiet space available in the home of the learner (as in CBT).

10. *"Lost in the Web"*. While surfing the Web, individuals often get lost in badly designed pages. Assuming that a WBT course has been properly designed, the navigation tools and site's structure will prevent this from occurring. However, the learner is responsible for remembering where she/he stopped when working on a particular tutorial or document. Very few Web-based systems have been designed to remember the learner's progress in a course, contrarily to CBT systems where it is a normal feature to "remember" where the user was last working, especially for those systems that use sequential and hierarchical presentation structures.

In addition, for communication supported WBT:

11. *Reliance on Electronic Communication*. Electronic communication has substantial advantages and is used extensively in everyday life for personal and business functions. Several theories such as Media Richness and Social Presence have analyzed the pros and cons of using electronic communication and discuss the problems that can arise from not conversing face-to-face in certain situations. Learners and instructors are all affected by the relative leanness of electronic communication tools. For example, will an instructor be effective in explaining a particularly complex problem to a learner via electronic means only? Another issue with using electronic mail as a means of communication, as discussed in the *Design* section above, is that messages related to the course can get mixed in with all other personal lists or junk electronic mail in the user's mailbox. Therefore, in times of required rapid response time, the mail that is lost in overloaded mailboxes will not be answered in a timely fashion.

Instructors

1. *Reliance on Information Service Provider*. Same issues that learners have.
2. *Increased Coordination*. Because several components are included in WBT courses, and because communication may need to be

incorporated into the course, the instructor is left with more coordination efforts than would be found in traditional class-room courses or in CBT.

3. *Digital Material Required.* Material that is to be used on the Web must be converted to digital format. For example, some topics that would be discussed verbally in class by the instructor now have to be either recorded (audio) or typed so they can be communicated to the learners. The same is true for diagrams that are often hand-drawn, which must be either redrawn with com-puter tools, or scanned in as picture elements (but which are then not easily modifiable). Substantial instructor time may need to be devoted to this conversion of material.

4. *Viruses.* Instructors are also at greater risk of "contracting" a computer virus when they exchange files with their learners on the Internet.

5. *HTML Knowledge Required.* Instructors who develop their own Web-based material can rely on a variety of easy to use tools (Internet assistants or Web development tools such as Microsoft's FrontPage® as discussed in the section on design and require-ments above). However, some knowledge of basic HTML may be required to debug problems with some on-line material.

6. *Dependence on Course Developer.* Instructors not wishing to be-come gurus at Web development must rely on the help of support personnel or programmers specifically assigned to help develop-ing WBT courses. The instructors run the risk of then becoming dependent on these individuals for modification, updates or problem resolution.

7. *Copyright Issues.* Instructors using material from several sources for their traditional lectures often borrow a table in one book, a quote in a magazine, and a diagram in another book. When these materials are digitized and grouped together on the Web, how-ever, the instructor has to pay even more careful attention not to infringe on any copyrights.

In addition, for communication supported WBT:

8. *Reliance on Electronic Communication.* Instructors face similar is-sues as learners with regards to electronic communication. Some of the issues mentioned in the section on communication facilities for WBT include the leanness of the media, the overload of

electronic mail messages and the possibility that they get over-looked in overloaded mailboxes, and the problem of response time when answers are needed rapidly.

9. *Authentication.* In a true cyber course, learners submit their assigned work electronically. The question of authentication is how to ensure that the individual submitting work or performing an exam is the actual learner registered for the course. This of course is only an issue when evaluation of learning takes place. Several training courses do not require any evaluations, so that the question of who is actually taking a course is less of a problem. The issue of authentication is often raised when discussing WBT courses, but how is it different than in traditional classrooms? Instructors can control having the proper students taking an examination, but they cannot control whether the student actually did the assigned homework on their own or whether someone else did it for them. Advanced methods of authentication (such as retinal scans or fingerprinting) are not yet cost justifiable in DL environments.

Institutions

1. *Reliance on Information Service Provider (ISP).* While learners and instructors may be upset with problems or performance issues with ISPs, institutions are also very dependent on these providers for ensuring that courses can be offered on-line to distributed learners.
2. *High Speed Network Connections Required.* High-speed connections are required between the organizations and their service providers. In addition, high-speed modem pools should be available for learners to connect to the organization's servers. These connections can be costly to implement and operate.
3. *Instructor Training.* Institutions wishing to fully embrace the Internet as a method of delivery for DL must be prepared to train the individuals who will be developing those courses, as well as individuals who will be moderating or delivering the courses. Substantial investments might be required for this training, or appropriate support personnel must be provided.
4. *Lack of Standards.* As there are a variety of tools used to develop WBT material (several of which will be discussed in chapter five),

there is no standard approach established. Problems exist if institutions adopt one particular way or tool for building their Web course environment, which then becomes obsolete on the market.

5. *Support Infrastructures*. Institutions willing to offer substantial levels of DL using Web-based approaches need a solid support and administrative infrastructure. This includes ensuring that proper backups are available, that maintenance is performed on regular schedules that will not affect learners and instructors, and that knowledgeable individuals are available at appropriate times to provide technical support to instructors and learners. If cyber courses are offered at any time any place, when is it an appropriate time for maintenance? (Only in between sessions?). Students often cram the night before projects are due, so what happens if network or server problems occur on that crucial evening? Will there be support personnel available at 2:00 in the morning to solve technical or administrative problems?

6. *Implementation and Operational Costs*. As already discussed there are substantial personnel for developing, maintaining and supporting the technology infrastructures. There are also important networking costs to support WBT courses.

Summary

Web-based training is gaining tremendous popularity in academic and commercial communities. It offers an instructional delivery technology for DL that is very suitable for learner-centric instruction. It has the capabilities of allowing interactivity between learners and instructors, but can also be used as an individual self-paced

Table 3.3 Summary of Requirements and Target for WBT Courses

Requirements			Target
Hardware	**Software**	**Other**	**Target**
• High capacity servers • Multimedia computers • Multimedia peripherals • Network connections	• High-end server software • Web development tools • Browsers • Networking packages	• Course developer or development support personnel	**Total conversion, combined delivery, or technology insertion** • Self motivated learners • Truly distributed learning environments • Learning requiring communication facilities

training environment. Therefore, it is best used for courses that are offered to motivated individuals wanting to learn on their own and who typically require minimal attention in traditional classrooms. It also offers a good alternative for courses where there are some communication requirements between learners and instructors. The danger of WBT is that there are so many different methods and tools for displaying information and integrating material that time can be wasted focusing on creating tools and pages instead of on teaching or training for the actual course content.

TELECONFERENCING

Description

Teleconferencing is a synchronous mode of distance learning that requires all learners in a course to be connected to each other (or to the instructor) for the duration of the session. Teleconferencing encompasses three types of conferencing technologies: audio, data, and video. Early forms of audio conferencing consisted of establishing telephone conference calls. These were not necessarily a good option for DL, although they could be considered to supplement video teletraining sessions (discussed in the following section) for remote learners to ask questions. Audio conferencing is performed using computer multimedia facilities such as microphones, speakers and audio software. Data conferencing includes all forms of simultaneous exchange of data between several individuals. This includes sharing documents to work on, automating file transfers to several individuals, and using chat facilities and whiteboards. When visual graphic and text data is complemented with audio capabilities, courses are said to use audiographic conferencing technologies. Finally, video conferencing uses cameras, appropriate multimedia monitors, and software to actually view remote individuals in a quasi face-to-face type environment.

Video conferencing can be implemented at two levels: large scale facilities and desktop video conferencing. Large scale videoconferencing is often implemented in large organizations that have set up specialized rooms and links to predetermined sites equally equipped for the sessions. Desktop videoconferencing is revolutionizing videoconferencing by providing access to its capabilities using personal computers and shareware, freeware or relatively inexpensive software over the Internet or local area networks. An example of desktop teleconferencing for training purposes is IBM's videoconferencing courses developed for their employees and delivered to their desktop workstations (Whalen and Wright, 1998).

A particular feature that must be considered in using teleconferencing facilities for DL is the type of interactivity that is available with the various combinations of technologies used. Three major categories of interactions should be considered when implementing teleconferencing: one way only (dissemination of information via audio, video, and/or text features to remote learners by instructors); two-way (allowing one-on-one electronic communication between the instructor and individual learners); and, many-way (allowing all learners to interact together and with the instructor or tutor via audio or video). Two-way teleconferencing is more popular than one-way because the instructor can deliver knowledge while receiving feedback from learners, individually. This is often implemented by using audio capabilities for feedback.

Requirements and Design

All forms of teleconferencing have one common requirement: a large bandwidth capability. Other requirements depend on the type of teleconferencing.

Large Scale Teleconferencing Systems

In courses that use large scale teleconferencing facilities, instructors must plan for specially designed rooms dedicated to this purpose to be available at all sites. These rooms need to be equipped with cameras (more than one if various angles and multiple participants from one site need to be seen at the same time), large screen displays, and some audio capabilities. Support personnel must also be provided. This represents a major investment to setup the facilities. It also means that this specialized room is typically used only for this purpose, a good thing if multiple courses are offered over time but not appropriate when few training courses are going to use teleconferencing technologies. Another major part of the investment, and this one is on-going, is the bandwidth requirement between the main training center and the satellite offices where remote education or training is broadcasted. The high-speed links between these offices typically use

Figure 3.2 Example of Teleconferencing Session
(Reproduced with permission from Microsoft Corporation)

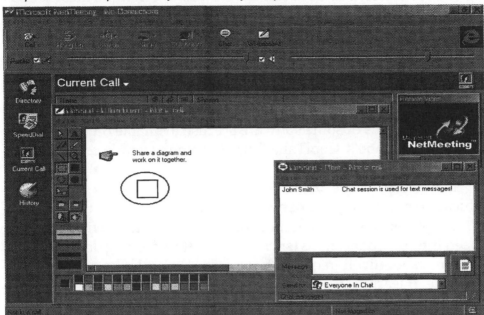

either satellite links or high speed leased communication lines such as T-1s and T-3s. The material for the course must be clearly presented using a combination of audio and video of the instructor, and some static material such as graphical or text material that can be shown to remote participants.

Desktop Teleconferencing

For desktop teleconferencing, the initial cost of implementation is much lower than for large scale teleconferencing. However, if several learners must be connected to the network for training purposes, the total investment can be substantial. Organizations often provide their employees with personal computers to perform their work. This investment can be leveraged by adding distance training as an additional application on the existing available technology. Learners must have access to a fairly recent and powerful workstation with multimedia capabilities (audio card, speakers, video card and monitor), and must be connected to a network.

To be seen and heard by others, learners must also have a digital camera (approximately US$ 120.00) and microphone (approximately

US$ 9.00). These tools are only needed for out-going audio and video signals. The user that does not have these can still participate in a session using data conferencing capabilities and can still see or hear others (if they have speakers and a proper audio card). The final requirement is to install a teleconferencing package such as Microsoft's NetMeeting® (http://www.microsoft.com/netmeeting/ for free trial) or CU-SeeMe (originally from Cornell University and now available commercially at http://www.wpine.com/). For audio only capabilities, free versions of some software are also available on the Internet such as Netscape's CoolTalk (http://home.netscape.com/navigator/v3.0/cooltalk.html).

If institutions are using teleconferencing for truly distributed education or training, the network of choice is currently the Internet. While learners could use data conferencing sessions with medium speed Internet connections (such as 28.8 KBPS), sharing documents to work collaboratively requires faster speeds or a lot of patience. For example, if learners work on a group project together, opening up a chat, whiteboard and sharing an application (such as Microsoft's Word® for word processing), wait time for control of the application can be a very frustrating experience for all involved.

Education or training via teleconferencing is still at its infancy, compared to large-scale videoconferencing, but its promises of geographic independence and low costs make it an alternative to seriously consider for future distance education and training programs.

Advantages

Learner

Face-to-Face. Teleconferencing systems that include a video component simulate face-to-face interaction. This is true for both large scale and desktop systems. Learners can view their instructors or other learners in real-time.

Learner-Learner Interaction. Learners learn from each other (as well as from their instructor). Therefore, teleconferencing systems that allow interactions between learners tend to improve the overall learning experience of all involved.

Learner-Instructor Interaction. Because learners have access to real-time interaction with their instructor, they can ask questions and obtain immediate feedback.

Geographic Independence. For desktop videoconferencing systems, learners can be geographically distributed worldwide. They can even take their courses from home. Large scale systems may require some small amount of travel for the learners. Teleconferencing nevertheless allows learners who would otherwise be unable to attend courses to learn or train in fields of interest to them.

Complex Problems Explained. Because teleconferencing systems typically allow the instructor to use a combination of audio, text, graphics and videos, complex problems can be explained to learners.

Instructor

Face-to-Face. While learners benefit from face-to-face interactions with their instructor and other learners, instructors also benefit from having real-time interactions with their students (for example, being able to determine if concepts have been clearly understood or need further explanations). Visual cues are also very important in reducing social loafing or lurking of learners at remote sites.

Complex Problems Explained. Instructors can explain more easily complex problems to remote learners by using the combination of audio, video, graphical and text capabilities of teleconferencing systems.

Ease of Revision. Because the material is delivered in real-time, the instructor can modify the content of the course as needed without wasting resources and requiring major efforts.

Institution

Operational Cost. If the organization uses desktop teleconferencing for training or education purposes, and it has already equipped its employees with personal computers the cost of providing this training is fairly low. Only teleconferencing software and network connections are needed. In educational settings, using desktop teleconferencing for education purposes shifts the cost of implementation to the learner who must provide their own computer, software and network connection.

Geographic Independence. By allowing any individuals with Internet access to use teleconferencing for education or training, institutions can reach much broader markets of trainees or learners than would otherwise be possible. Any individual worldwide could, in theory, register for a course and "attend" the classes.

Disadvantages

Learner

Bandwidth Requirements. For desktop teleconferencing, bandwidth requirements imply that learners will have their own high-speed connections to the Internet. In sharing applications, even large telephone system bandwidth (56 KBPS) may be insufficient for satisfactory response time.

Audio Limitations. Many desktop teleconferencing packages allow only two individuals to use audio capabilities at the same time. This means that each individual can only connect in audio to one other member of the group at a time.

Video Limitations. Just like for audio capabilities, many teleconferencing packages limit the interaction to be between two individuals at a time only.

No off-line work. Because teleconferencing sessions are held in synchronous modes, the learner must remain connected for the entire session, not being able to perform off-line work or connect only for needed interactions.

Instructor

Bandwidth Requirements. Just like learners, instructors connecting to teleconferencing sessions to deliver their material must have access to high-speed connections.

Audio and Video Limitations. Because instructors would typically like to communicate with all their learners, desktop teleconferencing can be severely limiting for them. Large scale teleconferencing, however, permits the use of video and audio on a one-to-many mode quite easily, allowing the instructor to deliver the material to the whole class simultaneously using audio, video and other capabilities.

Institution

Implementation Costs. For large-scale teleconferencing, the cost of facilities can be substantial since rooms must be built with large screens, cameras and communication capabilities. There must be several courses with a large number of total learners (over time) to justify these initial implementation costs.

Security and Privacy. In desktop teleconferencing, most organizations use the Internet as their backbone network. If such is the case, then issues of security and privacy of information that travels over this non-secured network can become important concerns for organizations. This is particularly true for training that deals with organization specific information of competitive advantage nature. Use of a company's intranet for training reduces some of these concerns.

Summary

Teleconferencing at a large-scale level requires a complex setup using video cameras and audio facilities. It is appropriate for small groups that use a set number of remote settings, and where remote learners can travel to the satellite site. The cost of the infrastructure is often prohibitive for organizations that have a limited number of courses to offer. If the interest is in having the instructor deliver the material synchronously without requiring interaction with learners, then video tele-training might offer a better alternative (discussed later). For truly distributed learners, however, desktop teleconferencing can offer a wide variety of advantages such as simulated face-to-face interactions between learners and instructors, and the use of multiple modes of learning (visual, audio and text).

Table 3.4 Summary of Requirements and Target for Teleconferencing Systems

Requirements			Target
Hardware	Software	Other	
Large Scale Systems			
• Large bandwidth connections • Cameras • Large Screens • Audio hardware	• Software to support connections, audio, and other systems	• Specialized support personnel • Special dedicated rooms	**Total conversion or combined delivery** • Small groups • Limited number of sites • Used often
Desktop Systems			
• Multimedia computers • Network connections • Cameras and microphones	• Multimedia software • Conferencing software		**Total conversion, combined delivery, or technology insertion** • For truly distributed learning

VIDEOTAPE

Description

This is one of the oldest forms of DL available, and it is still a very good alternative for several types of training and education. A well-known example of a training video used by corporations includes the one-hour video "In Case of Fire" used by Woolworth stores to train employees on how to react in case a fire flares up at the stores. Another is IBM's security training videos, alerting employees of the risks of industrial espionage and other security issues.

One of the characteristics of this type of training is that the delivery mechanism is quite simple: video projection equipment, screens and appropriate room. Sometimes, none of this is needed if the video can be sent out to employees' homes. Nevertheless, the material contained in the video should be of a fairly enduring nature, as it cannot be updated except for creating a new video (old clips can be kept while new clips are added). Videos are also linear and uni-directional in nature. This means that the learner is typically not active in the learning process since she/he is in the listening mode. Videos are often best used for DL when combined with other tools. For example, they can accompany self-study workbooks. They can also be digitized and used on computers in Computer-Based Training courses. This allows employers to deliver videos to employees in the form of computer disks that can be viewed on the employees' own worksta-tions (assuming that they support multimedia features).

Requirements and Design

Given the static nature of videotapes, it is particularly important to design them with a clear structure to facilitate learners' comprehen-sion and retention. Updates to videotaped material are not easily or cost effectively done. Therefore, material appropriate for DL courses should be of a fairly stable nature. The material should be organized in a way that provides first an overview of the course content, followed by an outline of the material to be covered in the course. This makes it easier for learners to have a global picture of what is to be learned and a clear thread to follow. Logical breaks should be in-cluded in the videotape to allow learners to stop as needed (in self-study mode) or for instructors to intercede information when combinations of modes of delivery are being used. Local requirements are limited since only a playback technology is required. This can be a videotape player or a computer with multimedia facilities if the videotape is digitized and sent on diskettes or CD-ROMs.

Advantages

Learner
1. *Temporal Independence.* Learners can follow a course at any time, and when it is more convenient or appropriate for them.
2. *Geographic Independence.* Videotapes can be easily distributed worldwide. Learners can take their courses at home or in their office.
3. *Limited Requirements.* Videotapes can be played back on any videotape player (except for incompatibilities between Europe's SECAM and U.S. VHS standards). As such, learners have no need to spend money on computer equipment to follow these courses. Of all the DL technologies discussed, videotapes are often the least expensive from the learner's point of view.

Institution
1. *Temporal Independence.* Videotaped courses require no instructors to be present when the learner takes the course. It is therefore easy to have the courses developed by an independent team of instructors and then distributed to individual learners.
2. *Scheduling Flexibility.* For courses that are taken sporadically by a large number of employees, videotapes can, like CBT courses, help avoid course scheduling issues.
3. *Overall Cost.* There is a rapid payback from the cost of producing courses delivered to a large number of employees or students. In addition, compared with instructor-led training, in videotape-only delivery, cost savings over time can be substantial since there are no instructor salaries and no travel costs involved.

Disadvantages

Learner
1. *No Feedback.* Learners taking videotaped courses receive no feedback on their performance (learning and comprehension) unless

the videotapes are accompanied by sets of exercises or tests to be taken and evaluated by instructors.

2. *One Mode of Learning Only.* Learners are passive when taking videotaped courses. Their only mode of learning is through visual and hearing reception of material.

3. *No Learner-Learner Interaction.* In videotaped courses, there is no interaction between learners.

4. *Lack of Instructor.* No instructor is available to help with difficult concepts when learners use videotaped courses.

Institution

1. *Difficulty of Revisions.* Updates of videotaped material require additional production costs often approaching the costs of the original product.

2. *No Control of Results.* Unless the institution incorporates testing tools with videotape training, there is no assessment of individuals' learning after they have taken the course.

3. *Learning Environment.* The institution or organization has no control over the learning environment in which the student or trainee is taking a course. Some home environments, for example, may be inappropriate for learning. If the videotape is used in poor settings, the material may also be destroyed (although multiple copies are usually available since duplication is easy and inexpensive).

Summary

Videotapes are still a very useful distance education and training alternative to be considered by organizations that wish to present a very specific topic that is relatively static in nature to a large number of learners. In a study of individuals who had the opportunity, but not the obligation, to take out training videos, Dobson (1995) found that employees are more likely to be positive towards the idea of taking those training videos if:

1. They think it has relevance to their job (in order words they expect some paybacks from taking the course);

2. They expect to receive recognition for their efforts (their managers would be supportive of their efforts to learn); and,

3. They believe it would increase their qualifications (or in other words they would get useful knowledge).

Table 3.5 Summary of Videotape Requirements and Target

Requirements			Target
Hardware	**Software**	**Other**	
- VCR or Computer		- Quiet learning space	**Total conversion or combined delivery** - Self-motivated individuals - Asynchronous learning - Large number of potential learners - Static material

VIDEO TELE-TRAINING

Description

Video tele-training (VTT) offers some of the facilities of teleconferencing and some of the facilities of videotaping. The technology involves using live video and audio capabilities to offer distance education or training at several locations. The instructor teaches a course in real-time that is being broadcasted to one or more remote locations, similar to remote broadcasting we see on television news channels. Learners can often participate in the course by asking questions using telephone lines or other two-way audio communication facilities. In remote locations, tutors or assistants are typically available to answer questions. Several large organizations use VTT extensively including academic institutions that have satellite campuses. The United States Air Force uses their own Air Technology Network (ATN) to deliver one-way video, two-way audio courses to every Air Force base in the United States. Another example is Hewlett Packard's' HP Interactive Network that is used to deliver courses to employees using two-way video and audio capabilities.

Requirements and Design

Implementing VTT requires special rooms at the main training center and all remote sites that are to be involved in the particular course. Understandably, there are substantial bandwidth requirements to connect these sites for transmitting audio, video and other data. Typically, organizations either use their own satellite links or high speed fiber trunks, or lease them for each session. Locally, the

Figure 3.3 Example of Equipment Setup for Video Tele-training
(Reproduced with permission of Virginia Tech's Institute of Distance and Distributed Learning)

instructor needs one or more cameras and at least two monitors. One of the monitors is used to view the outgoing video and one to view the incoming video. This implies that the instructor sees only one remote site at a time. In addition, the instructor needs to be able to use a set of integrated tools to display texts and graphics while being viewed and heard by learners at all sites. Video Camera Recorders, computer outputs, slides or other display tools can also be added to the set of integrated tools available to instructors.

The use of this technology means that technical personnel must be available to assist instructors for each course offered via VTT. At remote sites (and the local site if there are some learners there too), monitors must be installed to show the main signal and signals from other remote sites when learners take control (by using their microphones). If there are more than 10 learners, institutions should consider installing more monitors. Finally, the courses themselves should be designed to force some interactions between students while retaining some control. This will encourage camera shy learners to participate (and avoid completely dead time) while avoiding communication chaos.

Specific minimum requirements for setting up a VTT remote session include the following:

- Two or more television monitors (or computer monitors) at each site.
- One or more cameras at each site.
- Microphones for every participant if they are to have the ability to ask questions and participate in discussions.
- Network connections for transmission of signals to all sites.
- A CODEC (compressor/decompressor). This equipment allows the signals to be compressed and decompressed to improve throughput.
- A facilitator at all remote sites.
- Technical support personnel at all remote sites and the local site.

Advantages

Learners
Real Time. Because two-way audio communication links are typically available in VTT, the material covered during a course is in real-time. Learners with comprehension problems can obtain help right away, and the instructor can use visual inputs to reinforce explanations.

Up-to-Date Courses. Since VTT courses are given in real-time, instructors can modify the material as needed to offer the most current information to their students or trainees. Alternatively, instructors can repeat information when they get feedback that indicates comprehension problems do exist.

Interaction between Learners. Learners can interact verbally with each other between the various sites. This interaction can help learners learn from each other's questions and answers.

Interaction with Instructor. Learners are able to interact with their instructor verbally and sometimes in a simulated face-to-face when cameras are also installed at remote sites. This makes the course more personal for learners.

Instructors

Dynamic Updates. Since the courses in VTT are offered "live", instructors can modify the content according to feedback from the learners, or as important related events occur in the environment.

Interactions with Learners. Instructors can interact with learners to get feedback on course content and delivery. They also have more personal contacts with learners.

Institutions

Geographic Reach. Institutions wishing to extend their market of potential learners to remote locations can find that VTT offers this possibility. A course can be taught once in one location, and since it is distributed via video tele-training, several learners from several different remote locations can register for the same course and take it at the same time.

Operational Costs. When several large groups of learners are distributed in several remote locations, VTT can be a cost efficient delivery mechanism DL. Moderators, facilitators or assistants must be hired at each remote location, but they are typically paid substantially less than a qualified instructor is. In addition, the instructor does not have to travel to multiple remote, reducing travel costs that could quickly amount to substantial expenses for the organization.

Disadvantages

Learners

Scheduling. Most DL instructional technologies discussed in this chapter offer some form of self-paced study alternatives for learners. In VTT, however, learners must be present at exactly the time that a course is given, just like they would be for a traditional classroom environment.

Geographic Dependence. While VTT offers some DL capabilities, the infrastructure required to offer these courses imply that only a limited number of remote sites can exist. Learners must still travel to those sites. This travel may be substantially less than would be required if there were no DL facility, but it is still a constraint for the learners.

Visual Display Limitations. The monitors used in VTT are often simple large screen television monitors. These could be too small when there are several learners in a classroom, impacting the quality of what is viewed and heard by those learners that have to sit at a significant distance from the monitors.

Instructors

Scheduling. Courses must be scheduled in VTT since it is a synchronous delivery mechanism. When scheduling those courses, instructors must take into account potential time zone differences (when courses are offered globally). They must also allow sufficient pre and post course time for setup in the particular classrooms.

Increased Coordination. Implementing VTT requires substantial coordination efforts from the instructor who must manage local and remote learners' involvement in the course.

Difficult Participation. Some learners are camera shy while others become less inhibited when communication is mediated by technology. The instructor must carefully balance these two so that there are no total dead silences in class discussions and to avoid out of control and disruptive discussions.

Dependence on Support Personnel. Since VTT requires some audio and video production personnel, the instructor becomes dependent on their presence to ensure the smooth delivery of his or her course.

Institutions

Training Required. In order to efficiently use the facilities, each remote site must have moderators or assistants. These individuals must be trained (in addition to the instructor) to be efficient at facilitating learning in this environment.

Implementation Costs. The original setup costs to implement DL using VTT facilities can be substantial. Special rooms must be equipped with monitors, cameras, microphones and communication facilities. If there are few courses that will use the facilities, or if there are only small groups of students, these setup costs might take a long time before they are recovered. For such smaller groups, desktop videoconferencing might be a better alternative.

Production Personnel. VTT involves broadcasting technologies. Therefore, highly trained technical personnel are required for producing and supporting the courses, and must provide support for every session. If the organization does not already have access to this type of

Table 3.6 Summary of Requirements and Target for VTT

Requirements			Target
Hardware	**Software**	**Other**	**Target**
- Large bandwidth connections - CODEC - Cameras - Monitors - Audio equipment - Others as needed (PCs, VCRs, etc.)	- Software needed for running equipment as part of courses if needed	- Classrooms - Support personnel - Facilitators	**Combined delivery** - Medium size groups in few locations - That must meet regularly - Where communication and visual contact is important to course

personnel, costs are involved in hiring and training or subcontracting for those skills.

Summary

The appropriateness of video tele-training for DL is similar to that of large scale teleconferencing. A complex setup using video cameras and audio facilities is required, and the cost of the infrastructure can be substantial. However, larger groups can be taught at remote sites using almost basic classroom installations (plus monitors and microphones). It is a good alternative for institutions that wish to offer a large number of courses using video tele-training to several but limited number of remote locations. Institutions stand to gain in the long run and payback can be achieved within a reasonable time frame.

SUMMARY OF INSTRUCTIONAL TECHNOLOGIES

The ideal instructional technology for a DL program depends on the particular needs of the organization, as well as its financial means. In reality, however, the ideal technology may not be one technology, but rather a combination of the various tools described in this chapter. For example, distance learners could receive a CD-ROM containing the course material that includes Web-based links to material on an Internet site. The CD-ROM can contain most of the structure for the course and reference material, while the Web sites can contain any dynamic information that changes often, as well as communication facilities to "chat" with other learners taking the same course or tutors available to help with the material. Another example of combining instructional technologies is audiographic telecourses where students can hear prerecorded material while viewing related information (such as course outline and diagrams) on the Web (LaRose, Gregg and Eastin, 1998). These hybrid delivery mechanisms provide the optimum for DL students or trainees.

There are other important aspects of technology implementation to consider.

- *Equipment.* The equipment must be reliable so that learners and instructors don't find themselves in the middle of a session with a technology breakdown that prevents them from completing their course. Support must therefore be provided.
- *Support infrastructure.* Organizations must carefully plan a support infrastructure for remote learners that includes both technology assistance and course content assistance.
- *Ease of use.* When deciding which technology to use, institutions should pay careful attention to the ease of use of the particular instructional technology they are contemplating.
- *Cost.* Another factor that should be considered is the cost, of course, of implementing and reporting the technology as well as the cost to the user.
- *Interactivity and synchronicity.* Finally, issues of levels of interactivity and synchronicity, access to the technology, and ease of revision of the material by the instructor should all be thought through before a particular technology is selected. Important advantages and disadvantages of each technology described in this chapter and some key considerations are summarized in Table 3.7.

Table 3.7 Summary of Instructional Technologies and Some Key Requirements

	CBT	CAI	WBT	TC (large)	TC (desktop)	Videotape	VTT
Ease of use	H	M – H	M	M	M	H	M
Ease of revisions	L	M	H	H	M	L	M
Implement-ation cost	H	H	M- H	Very H	M – H	M	H
Operational cost	M	M	L	H	M	L	H
Geographic independence	H	M	H	L	H	H	L
Synchronicity	A	A/S	A/S	S	S	A	S
Interactivity							
- Learner: instructor L	M	M	H	H	L	M
- Learner: learner L	M	M	H	M	L	M
- Learner: content H	H	M	L	M	L	L

Legend: H: High, M: Medium, L: Low, A: Asynchronous, S: Synchronous.

Chapter IV

Media Conversion Analysis and Instructional Design Considerations

In chapter two, we discussed the different variables that impact suitability for DL. Chapter three provided the capabilities and limitations of technologies that can be used for distance and distributed learning. The purpose of this chapter is to provide guidance on the major steps involved in a media conversion analysis. They include the initial screening for DL suitability, determining what portion of the course is suitable for conversion, selecting the appropriate media for conversion, determining the number of hours required for development, pricing the cost of development and maintenance, and doing a benefit/cost or return on investment (ROI) analysis. Before beginning the discussion on media conversion analysis, a life-cycle model and approach to DL projects are outlined.

OVERVIEW OF THE ADDIE MODEL AND PROCESS

Instructional systems design (ISD) and development is a part of a lifecycle methodology that, if followed, will ensure that the systems that are designed are instructionally sound and effective for the purposes they were designed. The most commonly used model for the ISD process includes five phases: analysis, design, development, implementation, and evaluation, or otherwise known as the "ADDIE" model.

Analysis

The purpose of the analysis phase of instructional systems design is to ask, and answer, all the questions about resources, issues, and

Figure 4.1 ADDIE Model for DL Projects

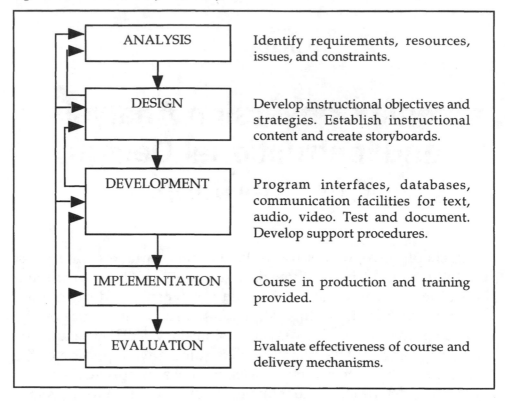

constraints that may impact the successful design and implementation of an instructional system. Some of these questions are basic, yet there are many projects that actually get launched without decision makers asking and obtaining answers to them. These questions are strategic and should be asked and answered before a media conversion analysis is conducted, which is presented in the following section.

Is there a business need for training?

Business requirements that are met by training include better on-the-job performance, increased safety performance, improved responsiveness to problems, improved attitudes or morale, increased understanding or knowledge of subject matter and increased or diversified skill set. Specific performance and functional requirements of the organization should be identifiable as being met with the planned training.

Who are the major stakeholders of this project, and who will be its champion?

Major stakeholders should be identified at the outset—users in the organization, technical support, human resources, training, managers, customers, outside vendors, etc. Each stakeholder group should be evaluated for how they might benefit from this project, and what (if any) objections they might have to it, and what 'hot buttons' they might have about the project. This exercise is highly useful if DL is not wholly embraced by everyone in the organization, or if there is a contingent of stakeholders who strongly prefer traditional classroom training. Understanding stakeholders' concerns, and being able to articulate an answer or response to their concern will increase your chance of successful design, development, and implementation.

What are the time and funding restrictions for the DL conversion project?

The answer to this question is critical, and it should drive the framework and timeline for the entire DL project. If decision makers do not ask and answer this question before the rest of the analysis is conducted, there may be an unreasonable expectation raised by the users, the designers, or other stakeholders. In a worst case scenario, the developer may be faced with an impossible situation where the users expect a full-blown interactive multimedia course within a short period of time, and senior executives are only willing to fund a fraction of the cost for the effort, and the technical support people do not intend to upgrade their antiquated hardware for several more years. What is a developer to do, short of giving up? Managing expectations as well as communicating realistic possibilities is a first step in the analysis phase. If no budget or time frames are explicit at the beginning of the project, there may be a request for an estimate of how much time and resources it would take to develop a course. In this case, the rest of the analysis questions will enable the designer to provide an estimate of the requirements, scope, cost of the project, and return on investment.

What are the goals and objectives of the training?

An example of an instructional objective for a course in business data communications would be to present concepts, terminology, examples, and business issues related to the use of data communications in the business environment. One goal of the course would be to have students, at the end of the course, be able to define the 7-layer open systems interconnect model of communications and to explain the functions and services associated with each layer of the model.

What are the user requirements?

What is the level of familiarity with different DL media? How does the system need to perform for the user? What is the best user interface?

(The next several questions can be answered as part of the media conversion analysis.)

What media is most appropriate to use for design and development?

The instructional objectives need to be examined to determine which media are most appropriate for instructional design. For existing courses that are being converted to a DL format, the results of the media analysis as outlined in this chapter would indicate which media are best suited for the instructional objectives in the course.

Are existing hardware and software platforms, and other technical infrastructures adequate for delivery of the instruction?

An assessment of your existing technical infrastructure, as outlined in chapter five, will provide you with an accurate picture of whether or not your existing infrastructure will support the chosen media for development. Based on the results of the media conversion analysis, you know what media types are suitable, and what your current technical infrastructure will support, and what hardware and software you need to upgrade it to your desired level of training infrastructure. If no additional technical infrastructure resources are available, or if technical upgrades will not occur in time for this conversion project, then you must plan your course content to operate on your current technology platform. For example, some organizational training programs are designed to accommodate employees' after-hour training at night or on weekends. Since most people have limited bandwidth capability from dial-up modems at home, developers must take this into consideration in the course design process. Another variable that designers must be cognizant of is the diversity of equipment platforms across an organization.

What is the estimated return on investment (ROI) for implementing this training via DL?

Chapter four outlines several methodologies for estimating your ROI for training. Senior decision makers are often very interested in this figure before making a commitment of time and money to a DL initiative.

What infrastructure investments in hardware and software will be required to execute this project?

If the organization is transitioning from a traditional classroom environment to an Internet or Intranet-based delivery system, or a VTT or TC based delivery, it must assess the infrastructure upgrades necessary to support these DL delivery mechanisms. Many organizations do not think of infrastructure considerations until fairly late in the game, which is a mistake because of the high cost of infrastructure investments. It is almost certainly the case that the support organization for Internet, LAN/WAN and desktop infrastructure is not part of the training services department. There should be participation from managerial and technical personnel in the technical support organizations on the conversion project from the earliest phases of the lifecycle, beginning with the analysis phase.

What types of training, education, financial, and technical personnel will be required to staff this project?

The issue of appropriate staffing is an important one that should be resolved before the project begins. If key stakeholders identify economic justification as an important rationale for undertaking the project, then the participation of a business/economic analyst on the project during the analysis phase is a critical success factor.

Is a pilot project or prototype development methodology appropriate?

There are several reasons that a pilot or prototype project might be a shrewd way to begin a DL conversion. First, the pilot represents an small initial investment in demonstrating and assessing the effectiveness of a particular type of DL delivery. There are many lessons that can be learned during the pilot or prototype, allowing the organization to make whatever adjustments it needs before a large-scale media conversion effort. Second, all organizational and change management processes that must be undertaken during a larger scale conversion effort can be identified, and exercised for this smaller pilot sample. A prototype offers the benefit of demonstrating functional and technical capability that users can experiment with, thus acquainting them with potential benefits of DL delivered courses, and giving them experience with new technologies.

Is there a user group within the organization that would be ideal to use as a pilot study group?

There are at least two philosophies regarding who should be selected to participate in a pilot study. One philosophy is to take a representative cross sample of the entire user base. The advantage of this approach is that you have a small sample of your actual population of users, so their reactions to the pilot is somewhat indicative of the larger population. One disadvantage of this approach is that, unless your pilot is very well designed and you know in advance from other indications (e.g., you are working with a knowledgeable, supportive user base) that it will have a high chance of success, you risk providing that same representative sample of users with a product that they find problematic—you now have "ambassadors" telling everyone that the system is not ideal. The other philosophy is to select a special subgroup of users to work with and use them to get a different kind of feedback. They may be a group of "power users" who will look at the prototype very critically and provide useful feedback on system design and functionality. They could be a group of subject matter experts who can critique the effectiveness of the system in achieving instructional objectives. They could be a group of learners who are most in need of remedial training, where an assessment of their pre- and post- participation performance could be analyzed. The rationale for whom should be selected to participate in a pilot study, or who should be invited to experiment with a prototype, should be guided by the organizational culture and its base of stakeholders, and the range and purpose of the type of feedback desired from the pilot or prototype.

Design

During the design process, instructional objectives are prepared along with evaluation metrics for learner performance and program evaluation. Subject matter experts provide input as the organization, structure, and sequence of instructional modules or objects are developed, including the logic and design flow of the instruction. Instructional strategies are developed to affect positive outcomes. For example, using an interactive character to motivate and interest learners, providing background information in an easily accessible way to promote self-discovery; providing simulated problems and role playing to enable learners to practice and apply what they have learned. Other examples of instructional strategies include computer games, collaborative exercises, and group discussions. The instructional strategies used will determine how complex the course needs to be, including the level of interactivity of the learner with the content, learner with instructor, or learner with other learners. Communication requirements (synchronous or asynchronous) are outlined. Once the instructional content and instructional strategies have been completed, the last step in the design phase is to create storyboards for the presentation of the instructional content.

Development

During the development phase all audio, video, and text materials are collected, prepared, or created. Interfaces requiring programming are developed, databases are created, including repositories for indexed and reusable objects. The complexity and bandwidth requirements for the learning objects to be developed should be within the capability of the technical infrastructure. For example, one would not produce extensive video clips for instruction if learners will take the course over the Internet using 28.8KBPS modems. During this phase the product is tested and documentation is prepared. Technical support procedures are developed and tested. Additional design and development issues will be discussed in chapter five.

Implementation

The course is put into full production during the implementation phase, including training both learners and instructors on how to use the different technologies involved. Further implementation issues will be discussed in detail in chapter six.

Evaluation

Assessment and evaluation is a process that should take place during the entire project. Different models of evaluation will be presented in chapter six. We now turn back to the issues surrounding a media conversion analysis.

UNDERSTANDING THE SCOPE OF THE MEDIA CONVERSION ANALYSIS

Much of the literature on DL technologies assumes that media analysis is conducted on a case-by-case basis—that an instructor or other decision maker is considering each course individually. In practice, many organizations need to consider dozens, or hundreds of courses at the same time for strategic planning purposes. Table 4.1 shows the advantages and disadvantages of project scope along two dimensions, size of sample and diversity of sample.

Advantages of Larger Scale Analyses

There are strong advantages for conducting a media conversion analysis on an entire curriculum or course inventory at the same time.

Long-Range Conversion And Investment Planning

DL conversion plans can be laid out for planning and budgeting purposes in order of priority. A time-phased conversion plan is practical since most organizations cannot afford to pay for conversion of an entire curriculum at once, and the imperative for conversion is not the same for every course.

Strategy For Reusable Learning Content

Assessing a large number of courses at the same time is a practical first step for identifying, organizing, and managing the reuse of instructional content among many courses. Learning modules can be developed, indexed, and warehoused in a repository during course design, development, and implementation. Chapter two discussed the concept of reusable learning objects as an objective.

Estimating Infrastructure Upgrade Costs

Infrastructure upgrades and other high-cost investments can be better estimated if many courses are evaluated at the same time. When examining the benefit-to-cost ratio (BCR), if the scope of analysis is too narrow (e.g. if only one or a few courses are being considered), the

Table 4-1. Matrix of Project Scope Dimensions

	SMALL INVENTORY	LARGE INVENTORY
WITHIN CURRICULUM	• Focused • Can evaluate both objectives and content • Can identify some commonality within curriculum • Develop/perfect methodology to roll out across larger inventory	• Requires greater level of effort, time • With proven methodology, can roll out efficiently in increments • Plan for learning object repository • Cost is moderate to expensive
ACROSS CURRICULA	• Must use high level factors, elements • Terminology issues across curricula • Diverse user base—difficult to understand and generalize user requirements • Difficult to generalize with small sample • Little commonality for reusable objects	• Must use high level factors, elements • Terminology issues across family groups • Diverse user base—difficult to understand and generalize user requirements • Requires great level of effort, time, money • Need to follow up with more focused look at content

infrastructure upgrades required may not pay off enough for those few courses. Many of the resources required to support one DL course are more cost-effective if the resources are used to support multiple courses at once. For example, it would be costly to lease T-1 service (1.544 MBPS throughput) line for Internet connectivity to support one course; it is less costly per learner if several courses share the bandwidth. On the other hand, T-1 capacity may not be enough once a certain threshold of courses is reached. Another example is the cost to produce a computer-based course on CD-ROM. The more copies are produced, the lower the cost per learner.

Disadvantages of Larger Scale Analyses

There are some disadvantages that begin to accrue if the scope of an assessment is too wide.

Increased Cost of The Analysis

Costs for a media conversion analysis increase as the number of courses evaluated increases, but at a decreasing rate, reflecting synergy of effort and some economies of scale. If there is a small, finite budget for media analysis with a large inventory of courses to evaluate, then the granularity of the analysis must be adjusted to these constraints. In general, given the same amount of resources to complete an analysis, the number of variables used in the screening process for media conversion analysis must be reduced as the number of simultaneous courses to be analyzed increases. As the granularity of the analysis becomes coarser, the degree of precision and accuracy of the analysis may be reduced. These are offset by the benefits of having a larger, more strategic assessment instead of a few data points. The critical variables for each segment of the analysis will be indicated in the narrative and in the summary charts; so that if resources are limited, those few variables can be used in the analysis.

Increasing Diversity of Variables

If courses from multiple curricula are examined, the diversity of the courses analyzed will greater. With increasing diversity comes a wider range of learning objectives, instructional activities, learning content, and perhaps a greater diversity of learner requirements. This diversity in the analysis makes it more difficult to define and apply a single set of decision criteria for conversion eligibility and media selection.

Ideal Scope for Media Conversion Analysis

The ideal scope for a media conversion analysis is one curriculum area at a time. Examples of individual curriculum areas include:

- Electrical engineering
- Accounting and finance
- Motor transport
- Environmental safety
- Desktop computer productivity tools
- Total quality management / quality control
- Management science
- Avionics
- Hotel management.

Each of these curriculum areas would contain many introductory, intermediate, and advanced level courses. Some courses would be qualifying or prerequisite courses for the others. In this ideal scope, the instructional content is related to the curriculum area; the infrastructure required to support the curriculum is easily identifiable

Figure 4.2. Analytical Hours for DL Evaluation for an 80-Hr Course

	course (1)	curriculum (15)	multi-curriculum (50)
☐ learning objective	12	153	570
■ course unit	8	96	360
▨ course	4	48	170

across courses; learning objects can be shared across that curriculum. Figure 4-2 provides a rough estimate of the number of analytical hours required to complete a media analysis depending on the granularity of the analysis and the number of courses to be analyzed.

Figure 4.2 is interpreted as follows. Granularity is rough if the analysis only considers course-level variables. The granularity of the analysis is finer if course units within a course are examined, and is the most finely grained if cognitive, psycho-motor, or affective learning objectives within each course unit are examined. For example, if only course-level variables can be considered, then it would take approximately four hours to assess an 80-hour course, assuming that all course-level data is readily available to the analyst. At the other extreme, if a course is evaluated at the level of learning objectives within each course unit, it would take more than 12 hours to complete an analysis for an 80-hour course.

In larger studies, particularly multi-curriculum courses, the data collection effort is substantial, and the data collection phase becomes a stage in itself in the overall analysis. In these large sample studies, we must plan, prepare, and execute survey materials, interview protocols, communication materials to explain (in a consistent way) the purpose, scope, and procedures being undertaken. In multi-curriculum studies, or large sample single curriculum studies, a "decision tree" should be developed to help analysts process each case (course) more efficiently. In large sample studies, the data will have to be aggregated and evaluated at the higher level (even if funding is available to examine learning objectives within course units) so that relative priorities can be set, and overall economic feasibility can be assessed. Usually in these larger studies, it is found that technology insertion cases end up with a lower priority than total conversion cases because the cost of technology insertion is high, and no savings can be attributed to learner travel, instructor costs, and other costs associated with traditional classroom training. On the other hand, technology insertion can be associated with huge cost avoidance if the technology (simulators, virtual reality modeling) replaces actual equipment that is significantly more expensive than the cost of the technology being inserted. An example would be personnel who train to be mechanics on an expensive aircraft. If they train on a real aircraft, the organization is incurring the cost of lost productivity represented by the aircraft and using an expensive piece of equipment that may be damaged during training. If the aircraft costs $2 billion (e.g., the B-2 bomber), then there would be a substantial cost avoidance by creating a virtual reality simulated environment where mechanics could learn to take apart (and break) "parts" of the aircraft.

THREE WAYS TO EMPLOY THE TECHNOLOGIES DISCUSSED IN THIS BOOK

Another implied assumption in the distance learning literature is that conversion to distance learning (DL) must be an all-or-nothing

Figure 4.3 Three Ways to Employ DL Technologies

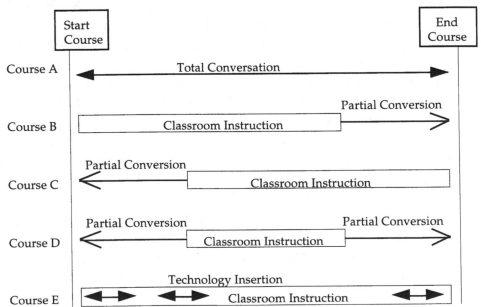

experience. As described in chapter one, there are three ways that the technologies discussed in this book may be employed, and many organizations evolve through these stages of technology use. First, several organizations will be interested in the use of instructional technologies within the traditional classroom environment as a natural first step, without commitment to replacement of traditional delivery with DL. We refer to this type of technology use as "technology insertion." Second, others may deliver parts of courses via DL, and part using traditional delivery, which we refer to as "combined delivery." Third, and most extensive, is the "total conversion" of traditional classroom training to DL. Figure 4.3 illustrates the three ways to employ DL technologies discussed in this book.

Technology Insertion in the Classroom

Technology insertion usually involves using asynchronous and synchronous communication and collaboration tools to supplement traditional classroom activities. It is most often implemented using CBT, WBT, or CAI. It has several benefits.

Enriched Learning Environment

Learners become part of a richer learning environment that includes the best of both worlds—instructor attention and the opportunity to practice and master tasks with CAI.

Direct Transfer Of Learning Into Operational Environment

Technology insertion using simulation tools helps with the transfer of learning directly into the operational environment.

Increased Acceptance of Advanced Instructional Technologies

The use of technologies in a traditional classroom setting gives instructors and staff time to learn and experiment with these technologies in a way that promotes greater acceptance, creativity, and confidence in the capabilities of these tools. It will also give instructional staff firsthand knowledge about what types of activities and situations are most effective in using these technologies.

Facilitated Collaboration

As computer-mediated communication and collaboration technologies continue to evolve, courses whose instructional activities and learning objectives require high levels of collaboration can be effectively met through the incorporation of these technologies into the classroom. As an example, consider the progress that these technologies have made over the past three years. Three years ago, many interactive, group oriented, instructor-led classroom activities could not be replaced with DL. Today, with electronic whiteboards, collaboration software, and desktop conferencing capabilities, groups of learners can interact with each other and the instructor in ways never before achieved.

Combined Delivery (Distance Learning and Classroom Activities)

If only part of a course is suitable for DL, we refer to it as "combined delivery," meaning that part of the course is delivered by traditional classroom methodology, and part of the course is delivered by DL without the presence of an instructor. Most combined delivery courses take the form of CBT, CAI or WBT with some teleconferencing support. It differs from technology insertion because the portion of the course that is converted to DL is delivered in place of traditional classroom instruction. Therefore, in addition to the benefits discussed for technology insertion which are also applicable to combine delivery, the main additional benefit of combined delivery is:

Shorter Overall Course Length

Combined delivery courses are shorter overall than the same course delivery in the traditional classroom. However, it is longer than the same course that has been totally converted due to the compression that occurs with conversion to DL. Compression rates for DL deliveries will be discussed later in this chapter.

Total Conversion to Distance Learning

If the entire course is suitable for conversion to a DL format, we refer to it as total DL conversion. In order for a course to be eligible for total conversion, there should be no course variables, instructional activities, or learning objectives that would be compromised by a total conversion to DL. DL delivery can occur in asynchronous or synchronous mode, and each type of delivery requires different tools and technologies to support it. Technologies appropriate for total conversion include CBT, WBT, videotapes, VTT and teleconferencing. There are many benefits of total DL conversion.

Increased Training Opportunities

DL provides increased training opportunities for students who are normally not free to participate in traditional learning environments. These include potential learners who live in geographically remote areas, learners with physical handicaps or disabilities that prevent them from having easy access to campus facilities, learners who have full-time jobs, military personnel who are deployed often, and parents with young children at home to care for.

Wider Access to Subject Matter Expertise

The DL environment provides learners with a wider access to subject matter expertise (through information systems as well as through human expertise) than is normally the case with a single instructor in the classroom.

Facilitated Sharing of Instructional Materials and Resources

From a pedagogical standpoint, DL allows instructional staff to pool their instructional materials and resources. For example, templates for course design, curriculum development, testing and evaluation, presentations, and other materials can be shared, including reusable learning objects.

Reduced Travel and Lodging

DL reduces learner travel and lodging costs associated with resident training or education. Instructor travel and lodging costs are also substantially reduced.

A summary of benefits is presented in Table 4.2. The next section discusses a three-step procedure for media conversion analysis. The first step involves screening for DL suitability. The second step is to estimate the instructional hours for total conversion, combined delivery, or technology insertion. The third step is to choose the most effective media types based on learning objectives, instructional activities, level of interactivity required, and types of assessments performed.

Table 4.2 Summary of Advantages of DL Technology Approaches

Technology Insertion	Combined Delivery	Total Conversion
Enriched learning environment	Enriched learning environment	Enriched learning environment
Direct transfer of learning in environment	Direct transfer of learning in environment	Direct transfer of learning in environment
Increased acceptance of technologies	Increased acceptance of technologies	Increased acceptance of technologies
Facilitated collaboration	Facilitated collaboration	Shorter overall course length
	Shorter overall course length	Increased training opportunities
		Facilitated sharing of instructional material and resources
		Wider access to expertise
		Reduced travel and lodging costs

SCREENING FOR DISTANCE LEARNING SUITABILITY

Before you go through the screening process, fill out forms A-1 and A-2 in Appendix A for each course you are analyzing. If you are analyzing a large number of courses, you should assign a unique identifier for each course. The following variables should be considered in the screening process for DL suitability—keep in mind that some variables make it less feasible for conversion to DL, while others make it more feasible to consider a DL delivery option.

Learner Throughput

As will be shown in the return on investment (ROI) section, courses that are scheduled frequently, and/or those with large numbers of learners are more likely to achieve a ROI sooner than courses that are scheduled infrequently or those with small class size. The total number of learners attending the course per year is calculated by multiplying the average class size by the course frequency to estimate learner throughput. Note that a better measure of throughput is market demand and the estimated demand for the course if there were no limitations of class size or course frequency.

Physical Risk

DL technologies are particularly suited for learning environments where there is some physical risk to the learner or the environment. Modeling and simulation software allows learners to make decisions, take the prescribed actions, and get the feedback on consequences of decisions/actions without real harm. Chemistry experiments, handling of biohazards, safe handling of explosive ordinance, and operating dangerous machinery are examples of learning environments where there is potential physical risk. Learners can learn the appropriate techniques, consequences of proper and improper procedures, and achieve mastery with no actual risk using DL technologies.

Recent advances in virtual reality modeling language (VRML) and computer-controlled robotics have opened up new vistas of training in psychomotor skills in individual and group situations. The technologies required to support effective instruction requiring psychomotor skills are highly technical and likely to be expensive. Therefore, they are often chosen for those types of skills that are very expensive to train under traditional means, and/or where physical risk of danger to the learner and others is high. For example, flight simulators train pilots by allowing them to make what would be fatal errors over and over until mastery is achieved. Surgical procedures can be taught to medical personnel that were previously only available through operating on cadavers. Using VRML technologies, complex, lifelike patient "responses" can be simulated, and the operating environment so well simulated so as to be identical with the real operating situation. However, unlike the real life situation, a surgeon can repeat a technique over and over again, and his/her psychomotor actions can be captured by computer technology for feedback purposes.

Hands-on Work/Activities

Despite tremendous advances in multimedia technologies, some learning objectives and activities are not adequately achieved without physical presence in the classroom of the instructor. Skills that are acquired through sensory experiences like touch and smell require hands on work. For example, learning diagnostic analysis in a medical checkup cannot be adequately learned without hands-on experience with real patients. Medical internships provide this opportunity as medical students follow doctors on rounds with patients and learn first hand the patient handling skills and diagnostic skills they need. A cooking class also requires physical presence, where students can smell, see, and experience the cooking preparation process. There are many cooking shows on TV, but a serious program of instruction for a cook would require hands-on activities and instructor guidance.

Use of Specialized Tools or Equipment

If training is required on specialized tools or equipment, then DL may not be appropriate unless (as in the flight simulator example), computer simulation is achieved with the specialized tool such that the skills required are exactly those required using the real equipment.

Group Training for Functional Teams

Two areas of training that are still beyond the reach of modern technologies are group-based psychomotor training and group-based interpersonal training. An example of the former is training fire-fighting teams. This type of teamwork requires split second timing, coordination, discipline and the ability to undergo physical stress (carrying a heavy and unconscious person down a ladder that is being pneumatically controlled by another fireman). Another example of psychomotor training is ballet. The group dynamics, plus individual psychomotor skills are important for real-life performance. Even if ballet students could look at computer-generated simulations of themselves at individual workstations, a ballet is largely based on the actual physical performance of the dancers, and no amount of "simulation" via computer will suffice, at least with today's technologies. An example of training in group-based interpersonal skills is facilitator training. In order to acquire the skills of a successful facilitator, one must have the opportunity to practice the nuances of facilitation in a real group setting.

Other Situations Where Physical Presence of the Learners and Instructors Are Required

There are instructional situations where the learning context requires the physical presence of the learners and the instructor. These include situations where group problem solving and instructor-guided and group discussions are required. As DL technologies evolve and mature, they will be able to support more of these activities.

VARIABLES TO CONSIDER IN CHOOSING TOTAL CONVERSION, COMBINED DELIVERY, TECHNOLOGY INSERTION

Once you have screened your courses and found that all or some of them are appropriate for one of the three types of technology use, the next step involves examining all instructional units within each course to determine the number of instructional hours eligible for total conversion, combined delivery, or technology insertion.

Psychomotor and Affective Learning Objectives

As chapter two described, affective learning objectives relate to learners' beliefs, values and attitudes towards situations, other persons, or the learning content. An example of an affective learning objective is "learners shall develop greater understanding and empathy for victims of discrimination." Affective objectives are difficult to quantify and even more difficult to assess. However, traditional methods of assessing affective outcomes usually require physical presence of, and interaction, with the instructor. An instructional unit with strong affective learning objectives may not be suitable for DL, but may be a good candidate for technology insertion. Psychomotor learning objectives are attained through physical performance of tasks that demonstrate knowledge of procedures, dexterity, speed, and accuracy. An example of a psychomotor learning objective is " learners shall be able to identify and safely disarm the explosive device."

Learner Performance Assessments

The method(s) of assessment may impact the degree to which DL technology can or should be substituted for traditional instruction. There are three models of performance assessment: continuous, periodic, and certification.

Continuous Assessment

In this model, instructors provide continuous evaluation and feedback of the learner's performance throughout the instructional activity. This can be accomplished in DL mode, but requires synchronous tools and communication software, and the effectiveness of the continual assessment depends on the richness of medium used in the interaction. An example of continuous assessment in a traditional learning environment would be a student driver and the instructor. Continuous feedback and evaluation is important both from the student's learning perspective and from a safety perspective.

Periodic Assessment

Periodic assessment may be handled either asynchronously or synchronously, depending on the complexity of what is being assessed. Typical asynchronous assessment methods include multiple choice, fill-in-the-blanks, short answer, essay questions, research papers, and individual projects that are turned in at a specific time. Asynchronous assessments are very easily converted to a DL environment. Periodic synchronous assessment includes individual oral presentations and group presentations of projects. Only a few DL technologies, such as teleconferencing, can handle synchronous assessment requirements, and the media richness of the technology may not be sufficient for an adequate evaluation. For example, it would not be effective to assess a concert violinist using teleconferencing; on the other hand, a topical presentation may be effectively presented via this technology.

Certification Assessment

This model involves taking an exam upon final completion of instruction (one course or an entire curriculum). Learners must demonstrate that instructional objectives have been met through achievement on the exam. Examples of certification assessments include the

Table 4.3 Learning Objectives and Assessment Type to Determine Technology Implementation Type

	Total Conversion	Combined Delivery	Technology Insertion
Learning objectives[1]	1,2,3	1,2,3,4,5	1,2,3,4,5
Assessment types[2]	2,3	1,2,3	1,2,3

[1]*Learning objective types:*
1=Cognitive
2= Software
3=Problem solving
4=Affective
5=Psychomotor

[2]*Assessment types:*
1=continuous
2=periodic
3=certification

Advanced Placement (AP) subject exams that high school students take upon completion of AP-level courses in high school; the Certified Public Accountant's (CPA) exam; and various computer technology certifications sponsored by vendors (e.g., Certified Network Engineer (CNE), for example). The certification model of assessment is itself asynchronous with the instructional process, and is suitable for many types of DL course delivery.

The tally on the Course DL Screening form in Appendix A shows the relative strength of the course as a candidate for DL. While any of these items individually would not disqualify a course from conversion, when they are accumulated, they may reach a point where the limitations of the course under consideration overshadow the benefits of course conversion.

VARIABLES TO CONSIDER IN CHOOSING APPROPRIATE DL MEDIA TYPES

Chapter three discusses four main categories of DL delivery. Each of the categories has several tools used for that type of delivery.

1. *Computer-Based Training and Computer-Aided Instruction.* CBT and CAI are included in a broad category of instructional delivery that can combine and integrate many different media, such as video, graphics, text, digital audio, animation, and interactive text. CBT/CAI is ideal for self-paced instruction, instructor-led presentations or on-the-job training.

2. *Web-Based Training.* WBT encompasses the use of instructional tools used over the Internet/Intranet, including listserv, e-mail, Web forums, multimedia over the Web, shared whiteboards, Web-based collaborative applications, virtual classrooms, etc.

3. *Teleconferencing Applications.* Teleconferencing applications include the use of video tele-training (VTT) and teleconferencing (TC).

4. *Videotapes.* Videotapes are included in a separate category that does not require the use of telecommunication facilities.

Deciding which primary delivery category is appropriate requires an analysis of course characteristics, learning objectives, and instructional activities to determine the most effective use of tools for that delivery category. Table 4.4, at the end of this section, can be used

Table 4.4 Summary of Variables to Consider in Media Analysis

Variable	CBT	WBT	VTT (and videotape)	TC	CBT/WBT Hybrid
Length of instruction >80 hrs	3	3	2	1	3
Class size	3	2	Limited	limited	2
Wide geographic dispersion of learners	3	3	2	2	3
Remediation / Learning to mastery	3	3	1	1	3
Group problem solving	0	2	1	3	2
Real-time instructor feedback/instructor-guided discussion/group discussions	0	2	2	3	2
Capture learner performance data	0	3	0	0	3
Automated course management information systems	0	3	0	0	3
Level of complexity	3	3	2	3	3
Temporal independence	0	2	2	3	2

3=fully meets criteria in functionality; 2=some restrictions in functionality; 1=possible but may not be effective; 0=no functionality for this requirement (does not apply).

to identify the most important variables to consider and can be used to evaluate which media are appropriate for an organization's DL environment.

Length of Instruction

It is important to evaluate the total number of instructional hours eligible for DL. In general, courses that are longer than 100 instructional hours are difficult to schedule, plan and deliver using some DL technologies. For example, scheduling of satellite uplink time, facility use, and costs quickly become prohibitive after the first 80 hours for VTT delivery. Longer courses are most suited for self-paced delivery using CBT or asynchronous WBT. A more practical solution is to consider which instructional units require live interaction via TC, or which portions of the course might benefit from VTT, while delivering the rest of the course using self-paced media such as CBT or asynchronous Web.

Class Size

For Web-based courses, class size is only limited by instructor resources and administrative overhead to manage each WBT course. A typical WBT course can accommodate hundreds of learners at any given time. The only limitation for WBT courses would be if synchronous activities are required, such as live chat forums or collaborative activities or projects. Under those conditions, smaller work groups can be formed ("cohorts") and small-group synchronous assignments can be assigned. In WBT asynchronous mode, the number of learners accommodated may be large, and they may in fact enter the course at different points in time. A "class" is not as meaningful for CBT courses, which are generally self-paced. The only limitation here is availability of the media (CD-ROM), access to multimedia-capable workstations, the CBT distribution mechanism, and any administrative overhead required to manage a CBT course. Class size becomes an issue for VTT and TC. In the case of VTT, class size is limited to the seating capacity of the classroom or auditorium where VTT is provided.

Geographic Location of Learners

If learners attending a course are co-located in the same building or within a corporate campus, training can be accomplished easily by several media (close circuit VTT, Intranet-based WBT, or CBT). However, if employees are located in countries outside the U.S., onboard ocean-going vessels, or if they travel frequently to many different locations in a short period of time, or if they do training from home, then CBT may be the only feasible medium for consistently available training. VTT and TC require access to training facilities, Intranet-based WBT requires access to the corporate Intranet, or Internet access, which may not be adequate in some areas outside the U.S., or aboard vessels at sea.

Geographic location of learners is important for another reason. If learners travel from many different locations to the training site, the organization may incur the cost of travel, lodging, and other costs associated with transporting the learners to that site. The time spent at the learning site also represents a loss of productivity for the employee at his or her work place.

Remediation / Learning to Mastery

If learning objectives require a learner to achieve 100% mastery at completion, then learning is best accomplished using self-paced media where remediation can be conducted at the learner's pace. VTT and TC are not suitable for learning to mastery because the dynamics of the group in TC, and the broadcast schedule in VTT are less conducive for accommodating a learner's need to repeat an action or lesson until 100% mastery is achieved. Learners may need to review course materials or complete course activities for remedial reasons. Course content in some courses is such that one must achieve full understanding or mastery in previous learning units in order to proceed to subsequent units. The synchronous technologies (VTT, TC, and live Web forums) do not make it easy for learner remediation. Asynchronous technologies (WBT, CBT, CAI and videotapes) allow the learner to go back over instructional materials for remediation.

Group Problem Solving

Group problem solving is benefited by both asynchronous and synchronous technologies. When a group of learners is involved in problem solving, asynchronous communication allows participants time to "go away and think about it" and return to the problem when they are ready to work on a productive solution. Working in asynchronous mode allows them to participate at their own convenience, and to evaluate the input of others over a span of time. On the other hand, some types of problems (e.g., wargaming, advertising development, computer animation) may benefit from multiple participants interacting at the same time through collaborative tools. The level of complexity of the problem, the characteristics of the learners (novice, expert), and the expected outcomes (product, idea, solution) must be considered to determine the appropriate DL technology.

Instructor Feedback / Instructor-guided Discussion / Group Discussion

The purpose, content, and length of instructor feedback, instructor-guided discussions, and group discussions should be considered to determine whether synchronous or asynchronous technologies are most appropriate. If the discussion topic is controversial, complex, and if the dynamic of the group is also important, then a rich communication medium is needed, such as TC. If the discussion is less complex, or if the group dynamic is not as critical, then VTT with two-way audio may be employed. If the learning objectives are closely tied to continual interaction between instructor and learner, and if instructor feedback is critical to accomplishing learning objectives, then synchronous DL technologies are required. Group discussions can take place asynchronously as well as in real-time. Threaded discussions using a listserv, e-mail distribution, or bulletin board document participants' communications in a sequential manner but do not occur in real time. Desktop teleconferencing applications such as Microsoft NetMeeting® enable participants to have a group discussion using a desktop video-camera and software while allowing participants to collaborate on the application through shared mouse control.

Capturing Learner Performance Data

If learner performance statistics or records must be kept, then WBT is the most useful media because the learner's responses and actions can be captured through the use of "cookies," and statistics can be kept in server-side applications known as course managed instruction (CMI) or course management systems (CMS). Few statistics can be kept about a learner's performance during a VTT session, even with two-way audio, except notes kept by the instructor of a learner's responses to direct questions. Qualitative assessment can be made of a learner's performance in a TC session, but no automated tracking is possible. CBT systems can track a learner's answers and performance on tests, but these are not captured at a centralized server for administrative purposes.

Course Managed Instruction

Well before the number of DL courses supported by an organization increases, the learning institution needs to plan for an effective way to administer course registration, learner tracking, curriculum design and management, and support for an online course catalog. Stand-alone or broadcast instructional systems (CBT, VTT, or TC) do not permit the automating of these processes in a seamless way with the course delivery systems, but WBT and hybrid delivery systems can create a comprehensive yet virtual campus environment.

Course Management Systems

Course management systems (CMS) is an emerging category of support tools, defined as enterprise software, implemented and integrated into administrative processes (often called "back-office" systems) for the creation and management of an on-line learning environment. CMS contain the functionality in CMI with additional capabilities that allow instructors to create on-line courses from word processing, audio, video, and presentation files. Top performing CMS also include advanced CMC (synchronous and asynchronous) functions for learners, instructors, and other staff, and assessment and reporting functions on learner performance. Users, instructors, course creators, and systems administrators can access CMS anytime, anywhere through any Web browser. CMS are considered "turn-key" solutions for implementing a virtual campus environment. A key point is that CMS can support physical, campus-based learning institutions, or they can help create virtual campuses. CMS should be designed using nonproprietary technologies, be locally installable or centrally managed, be highly scalable, support integration with other virtual campus systems, and support third-party authoring tools and learning materials. The use of CMS will provide a return on investment in three ways:

Lower costs for instructional delivery. Research on CMS implementations suggests that labor accounts for over 70 percent of current operating costs in institutions of higher learning. Studies show that investments in academic computing, such as CMS, can reduce the labor portion of the budget by about 4 percent for a traditional lecture-based course, and by 16 percent for a course remotely delivered using instructional technology.

Improve staff productivity. CMS provide point-and-click support for building a course from existing learning materials (video, graphics, text, audio, presentations), which can save a significant amount of faculty time. The automated functions of a CMS for testing, grading, making announcements and reporting also save faculty time and allow them to be more productive overall.

Serve more students. Extending the campus beyond the reaches of a resident schoolhouse can increase student throughput, particularly in cases where there is a backlog of learners needing a course (e.g., National Guard and Reserve backlog).

Improve course quality. The educational advantages of using CMS include enhanced learner-to-learner and instructor-to-learner communication, learner-centered teaching, around-the-clock access to course materials, anytime evaluation of student progress, and more effective use of classroom hours (for CMS that supplement traditional classroom environments).

Typical features of a high-performing CMS would include:
- Course calendar with announcements

- Asynchronous communication (threaded discussions)
- Synchronous communication (chat rooms and shared whiteboards)
- Course study groups
- Messaging system (e-mail) and on-line file exchange
- On-line tutorials
- Automatic sequencing of linked course documents
- Application customization for the "look and feel" of a particular organization
- Content reordering and searching capability
- Course navigation functions
- Content creation and distribution capability using third party authoring systems
- Instructional design tools
- On-line course migration tools to package and install on other servers
- Scalable for use on an enterprise basis across schoolhouses.

Level of Courseware Complexity

Course complexity is sometimes a surrogate for level of interactivity. In interactive multimedia course development, there are three levels of complexity. **Level 1** courses are composed of text and graphics; **Level 2** includes interactive text and graphics; **Level 3** includes video, sound, animation, and interactive text. The factors that influence the required complexity of the courseware include:

Technical infrastructure available to the learners

The level of courseware development should not exceed the ability of the population of learners to access the courseware. If the learners are dialing in from home on relatively low-speed modems, then downloading large graphics and other large multimedia files will present a problem.

Level of engagement required during learning to achieve learning retention

Some topics require more engagement from the learner in order to be effectively presented. For example, if learning objectives include both cognitive and affective dimensions, then a higher degree of engagement is required. This can be accomplished by designing higher levels of interactivity between the learner and the courseware.

Complexity of the topic

The use of multimedia and level 3 courseware may be required for topics that are complex—for example, the presentation of learning content for a course on quantum physics would be most effective if we could see a video and animation of the behavior of quanta, light, and energy. The animated video would provide the student with a more intuitive understanding of the set of equations and text that explain the topic. The course would also benefit from high levels of interaction between the learners and the teacher, so that examples, question and answer, and additional explanatory material could be provided to learners on an as needed basis.

What level of learning objectives must be achieved?

In the cognitive domain, active problem solving activities require higher order cognitive activity such as analysis, synthesis and evaluation. These higher order cognitive activities require more sophisticated courseware to achieve learning objectives, to retain learning, and to maintain interest and engagement of the learner.

Degree of simulation required

Courses that require simulation of interpersonal situations, or bringing to life historical events may require more sophisticated, level 3 courseware. For example, a highly effective training course on customer service might include a simulated environment where the learner is presented with customer problems in a simulated environment. A video would show the learner taking a trouble call, dealing with a difficult customer, doing research to resolve the issue, and completing follow up documentation to process a customer complaint. The courseware could be highly interactive, showing different "outcomes" based on the learner's actions and decisions.

Temporal Independence

As discussed in chapters two and three, DL instruction can be delivered in synchronous (real-time) or asynchronous (non-real time) mode. In synchronous delivery, learners and instructors participate in the learning process in real time. In asynchronous delivery, they can communicate sequentially at their own convenience.

EVALUATING INSTRUCTIONAL UNITS

An instructional unit is defined as a group of lessons or modules that are integrated to complete a usable skill, knowledge or to aid in scheduling a course. An instructional unit is a basic component of courses, which can be developed or converted into a learning module for DL delivery. This is the basic unit of reuse, which can be combined, integrated, or rescheduled within a course. These are examples of instructional units within a hypothetical data communications course:

- Local area networks and protocols.
- Wide-area network functions and services.
- The 7-layer Open Systems Interconnect (OSI) model.

Each of these instructional units would have several lessons or chapters associated with it, an overall unit exam, and possibly several smaller tests or quizzes. As an instructional unit, it is modular and could be scheduled in any particular order in the course.

When Form A-3 (Appendix A) has been completed, examine all instructional units to determine if any of the units have objectives or course level variables that prevent the entire course from full conversion. Add up all the hours for instructional units that cannot be converted. The total hours for the remaining units can be considered for conversion using one or more media. If the course has particular requirements that mandate the continued presence of the instructor and learners, then instructional units can be considered for technology insertion.

Note that the instructional activities, type of learning objectives, and type of assessment in Form A-3 are listed in relative order of suitability for DL conversion. The media choice types are listed in order of relative level of interactivity and synchronicity.

ESTIMATING COMPRESSION RATES

When traditional classroom instruction is converted to a DL format, there is a "compression factor" that takes effect because the amount of time required to present the material is shortened, or "compressed." There are several reasons why DL courses are relatively compressed, compared with traditional classroom delivery.

1. DL courses must be carefully designed and programmed. As a result of the ADDIE process, much of the "fat" in instructional time is removed—the jokes, "warm-up" by the instructor before the lecture begins, the socializing when learners come up just before or after class to ask questions. These all take place in DL under technology-supervised conditions, and therefore tend to be more task-oriented than face-to-face socializing. This is a reason why a real-time delivery method like VTT or videotape has a compression factor. Many people assume that since the instructor is speaking at the normal rate of speech, that there is no compression associated with VTT or other TC methods of delivery. The "compression" of overall course length is actually the result of better and more frugal use of allocated satellite time for VTT and TC systems through careful planning and avoidance of unnecessary chatter.

2. Content delivery with multimedia DL technologies allows for a faster pace of learning through multiple sensory modes, a more holistic learning process, and overall compression of learning time. As the saying goes, "a picture is worth a thousand words." In the time it would take to read, process and learn a complex theory, a well designed and directed animated visual simulation can vividly illustrate the process. This type of compression is typical of WBT and CBT courseware.

A compression rate is represented as a percentage, and is calculated as follows:

$$H_{CD} - [H_{CD} \times CF] = CH$$

Where H_{CD}= Hrs of classroom delivery, CF=Compression factor (%), CH=Compressed hours.

For example, it is estimated that a compression rate of 35% can be achieved with Level 2 (interactive text and graphics) WBT. This means that for a traditional classroom delivery that takes 100 hours, the same material could be presented in WBT Level 2 format in 65 hours. DL media have different compression rates, as described in Table 4.5.

ESTIMATED DEVELOPMENT HOURS

Development hours are presented as a ratio of the number of hours it takes to develop one hour of instruction. Development hours

Table 4.5 Media Compression Rates

	Compression factor	Development Hours		
		Level 1 (low)	Level 2 (medium)	Level 3 (high)
CBT	35%	50	265	700
Intelligent CAI	35%	250+	600+	1000+
WBT (Level 1)	25%	50	-	-
WBT (Level 2)	35%	-	265	-
WBT (Level 3)	35%	-	-	700
WBT (Synch)	0%	50	265	700
VTT	20%	10	90	250
Videotapes	20%	10	90	250
TC	25%	10	40	80

are provided for Level 1, 2, and 3 courseware, as described by "level of complexity" and calculated as follows:

$$CH \times DHI = DHR$$

Where CH=Compressed hours, DHI=Development hours per hour of instruction, DHR=Development hours required.

For example to develop a highly complex 40-hour Level 3 CBT course (which reflects a compressed 54 hour class), (40hrs)(700hrs) = 28,000 hours of development time is required for the project. The development time represents tasks for all phases of the ISD lifecycle, as reflected by the ADDIE model presented at the beginning of this chapter.

Note that these are very rough and general estimates for development times. Among professionals who manage such projects, estimating development hours for a conversion project is both a science and an art. Actual development times vary, depending on several factors, each of which can add to project risk as well as lifecycle costs. Table 4.6 lists these risk factors.

RESOURCES REQUIRED THROUGH THE CONVERSION LIFE CYCLE

A course conversion project encompasses all phases of the ADDIE model—analysis, design, development, implementation, and evaluation. The estimated relative level of effort expended at each phase depends on the level of instructional complexity to be developed. The chart (Table 4.7) provides an estimated level of effort for typical

Table 4.6 Factors Affect Project Risk and Lifecycle Costs in Courseware Conversion

Factor	Project Risk	Lifecycle Cost
Lack of senior management support for the project	x	
Lack of strategic training plan	x	x
Lack of adequate resources to fund a media conversion analysis, which should ideally be done one curriculum at a time	x	
Lack of communication/marketing effort to obtain approval and support from all major stakeholders, particularly in multi-curriculum conversion initiatives	x	
Lack of subject matter experts (SMEs) for all courses under evaluation; and for courses under conversion	x	x
Lack of good course documentation (syllabi, learning objectives, testing materials)	x	x
Lack of electronic versions of existing course content (lectures, graphics, photos)		x
Lack of commercial sources for video, audio, graphic content		x
Lack of in-house staff who are available and have technical conversion skills (authoring systems, web tools, graphics arts)		x
Lack of a well-thought out architecture for how to identify, define, index, store, and retrieve reusable learning content	x	x

Table 4.7 Estimated Conversion Time for Each Step of ADDIE Process by Level of Complexity

Level of complexity	Analysis	Design	Development	Implementation	Evaluation
Level 1	5 %	15 %	75 %	4 %	1 %
Level 2	5 %	20 %	70 %	3 %	2 %
Level 3	10 %	25 %	55 %	5 %	5 %

conversion projects. Some generalizations can be made.

In general, as projects become more complex, more time is spent in the analysis and design phases. Existing text materials and graphics must be redesigned for interactivity, motion, and sound. For Level 1 conversion projects, if course content already exists, the bulk of effort is spent in development. Level 1 courseware is text and graphics, and traditional course materials are easily converted and may not have to be designed from scratch. Note that some resources must be set aside in a project for implementation and evaluation. There are three ways to staff a conversion project: freelance, contractor, and full-time. There are advantages and disadvantages with each approach (Frenza and Szabo, 1996).

Freelance Conversion Support

Freelance support is typically paid by the hour. If you are experienced in course conversion, understand the entire process and intend to manage the project yourself, and have skilled analysts to work through the analysis and design phases, you might consider freelance support for the courseware conversion.

Advantage: When you hire freelance support, you only pay for what you need. As Frenza and Szabo (1996) note, "You get what you pay for, and you only pay for what you need."

Disadvantage: It is difficult to find highly skilled people who can jump into the middle of your project, provide exactly the help you need and make an immediate contribution without some guidance. If you do not have everything structured and organized, then you will waste both your time and the freelancer's time trying to figure out "what you need." The pricing of freelance work may be difficult or risky, if payment is based on an hourly rate rather than fixed price or piecework.

Contractor Conversion Support

Contractor support can be obtained on a time and materials (T&M) basis or fixed price (FP) contract. It is desirable to specify the scope, products, and criteria for acceptance of the project, with an estimate of the level of effort embedded into the contract. In FP contracts, the client must know what is to be done, what is included in the outputs, and what criteria will be used to determine acceptability. If your project specifications are not clearly outlined in the Statement of Work, there will be unresolved issues between expectations of the client and the contractor.

Generally, a well-qualified and experienced contractor will be able to provide sample statements of work and cost estimates for other projects of similar scope. You will be able to estimate the level of effort for those projects and your own and come up with the ballpark estimate of the cost of the conversion. If this information is not available, if the scope of effort is not clear, then consider a T&M type of contract.

Advantage of T&M contract: Similar to freelance work, you get what you pay for, and you pay for what you get.

Disadvantage of a T&M contract: The disadvantage to the client is that there is no "burden" put on the contractor to be efficient in completing the project, and it will be difficult to assess the final cost of the project.

Advantage of a FP contract: In a FP contract, the client knows up front exactly what is contracted for (results, output) and how much it will cost. The contractor can often make a good profit on a well-estimated and well-managed project.

Disadvantage of FP contracts: The disadvantage of a FP contract to the contractor is that it is difficult to assess the scope of the project ahead of time unless they have done this many times before and understand the client's needs very well. Also, there are always unforeseen difficulties on the project and any change in cost due to client-related reasons, or unforeseen circumstances require a change or modification to the FP contract.

Full-time Conversion Support

The decision to hire full time conversion support requires a commitment by the organization to retain the services of these employees on a full-time basis. If the conversion involves only a few courses, this may not be feasible. Also, the types of skill sets and personnel involved in a conversion project are diverse. If the organization is not a high tech firm, these personnel will not "fit" into the human resource pool of the rest of the organization. If course conversion is a one-time initiative (with maintenance afterwards), then it should be treated as a project and hiring full-time personnel for this has more disadvantages than advantages. However, if the organization is a large education or training facility with instructional activities as a core line of business, then it would make sense for them to plan, organize, and establish a course design and development capability.

Advantages of full-time support: The organization has total control over the selection of personnel on the project and has direct control over their reward system. Personnel are engaged within the larger organization and, hence, should be more familiar with organizational norms, processes, and hopefully, the knowledge/learning needs of learners in that organization.

Disadvantages of full-time support: DL conversion projects are similar to construction projects. Most organizations would not hire their own full-time construction staff for building a new wing, but would contract the work out. An exception might be a construction firm that is itself adding an extension to their building. Likewise, if multimedia courseware development is not a core competency of the firm, nor its mission, taking on a full-time staff is a large, long-term commitment. The scale of the conversion effort may determine whether this is a feasible idea or not.

Media Conversion Project Roles, Responsibilities, and Costs

For even the smallest conversion project, you need people with project management, analysis and design, programming, graphics, and production experience. Some of the first questions that executive decision makers ask of the human resources development (HRD) department is, "What will this project cost?" "What is the benefit of undertaking this project?" "What is the return on this investment?" The first two questions should be asked and answered in the analysis phase, where all major stakeholders in the project should be identified. This is a critical time when senior decision makers, learners, and instructors identify and evaluate their expectations, constraints, and available resources in the context of organizational strategy in general and training strategy in particular. There are three cost modeling techniques that can be applied to answer these questions: life cycle training costs, training benefit to cost analysis, and return on investment analysis.

Life Cycle Training Costs

Project costs from inception through completion must be planned, budgeted, and tracked. A lifecycle approach to tracking the value of training investments can be used by organizations that seek to show cost savings achieved in DL conversion. Using this approach, a comparison of alternatives whose benefits are perceived as equal is evaluated. Therefore, the potential savings of alternative DL solutions are compared with the costs of the traditional training delivery. The steps in this process are:

- Establish baseline lifecycle costs of your existing training programs.
- Identify DL media alternatives that are feasible given learning objectives, instructional activities, and other course requirements.
- Estimate life cycle costs for each alternative.
- Compare life cycle costs of feasible alternatives that provide the same instructional quality.

The costs of training systems should be tracked throughout its lifecycle. Cost elements in each phase of the ADDIE model should be identified so that the total cost of training can be estimated for existing training and for the proposed DL conversion project. The relative level of effort and resources required for each phase of the life cycle can be roughly estimated for the complexity of the course. Course complexity is often used as a surrogate measure for level of interaction.

Table 4.8 Courseware Conversion Project Roles and Costs

Role	Annual Cost	Hourly Rate
Project Manager	$55,000 – 95,000	$35 – 50
Creative designer	$35,000 – 65,000	$20 – 60
Illustrator / graphics artist	$40,000 – 50,000	$35 – 50
Editor	$35,000 – 65,000	$15 – 25
Photographer		$40 – 100
Animator / 3D	$40,000 – 60,000	$60 – 100
Audio engineer		$20 – 35
Videographer (cameraman)		$45 – 100
Programmer, C, CGI, Java	$45,000 – 120,000	$50 – 100
Subject matter expert	$50,000 – 100,000	$50 – 125
Other Conversion Specialists		
Instructional designer Instructional developer Production & distribution support DL site administration Course scheduler/registrar Evaluation support Quality control Courseware developers	Content editor/writer Illustrator Photographer 2D/3D animator Sound editor/composer /musician HTML/CGI programmer Webmaster Graphics artist Help desk	Instructors VTT moderators, scheduler, and producer/director Videographer Audio engineers Media specialist Production assistant Systems / server administrator Authoring specialist

Some of the cost elements of traditional training are the same for conversion to DL technologies. If the course content has been developed for traditional delivery, then there will be little or no effort in the analysis and design phases, and most of the work will occur in the development phase. Course conversion involves additional roles and responsibilities compared with traditional instructional design.

Benefit-Cost Analysis

A benefit-cost analysis quantifies both the costs and the benefits of non-comparable alternatives. Some people refer to this as comparing the "cost of apples with the savings from oranges." The formula for a benefits to cost ratio is:

BCR = <u>Program benefits</u>
       Program costs

The BCR is a ratio of the present value of development and recurring costs to the present value of benefits. Costs and benefits should be estimated over a life cycle that is long enough to capture program benefits and is consistent with long-range planning cycles for the organization. For example, the federal government's program budget cycle is six years.

Steps in a Cost Benefit Analysis: The four steps in a cost benefit analysis are:
- Assess the current costs of training.
- Identify training alternatives using different delivery methods.
- Calculate training benefits.
- Assess life cycle costs and performance outputs.

Figure 4.4 Lifecycle Costs of Distance Learning Alternatives

LIFECYCLE MAINTENANCE COSTS	INITIAL CONVERSION COSTS	
	HIGH	LOW
HIGH	VTT, TC (no facilities in place)	VTT (with facilities in place)
LOW	WBT, CBT, HYBRID	VIDEOTAPE

Types of Training Benefits: The most common types of benefits identified in DL conversion include:

- *Cost Savings.* These include savings in the cost of existing training as a result of course conversion. Examples of savings in this category include the cost of instructors; cost of learner travel and expenses; and cost of building facilities and maintenance.
- *Cost Avoidance.* This type of benefit is one that is realized by deferring or avoiding costs from existing training programs. Examples include avoiding the cost of constructing a new building to accommodate increased learner demand; or, avoiding loss of life through training.
- *Non-quantifiable Benefits.* Don't forget to identify qualitative benefits. These may be non-quantifiable, but they may also have been the imperative for pursuing DL in the first place. Examples of non-quantifiable training benefits include providing training for learners who do not have access to traditional classroom training; or, improving morale in the workforce.

Types of Training Costs: The most common types of costs associated with DL conversion include:

- *One-time Course Development.* The one-time costs to develop DL courseware in one of the alternative delivery methods (e.g., WBT, CBT, VTT). Courseware development includes costs for each of the lifecycle steps identified in the ADDIE model.
- *Recurring Course Refreshment.* Course refreshment includes the cost to update course content or the tools used to maintain courseware.
- *Infrastructure upgrades.* The costs of upgrading computer hardware, software, networks and other equipment for training development or delivery should be included.

Return on Investment (ROI) Analysis

In order to show that expected benefits from training have been realized, organizations must show improvements in performance. There are several reasons why this is a challenge. The overall impact of training initiatives may not manifest itself for several years. It may be difficult to quantify all the benefits, and some benefits can only be measured indirectly. In order to measure results, we must understand four types of outcomes that result from training. Kirkpatrick (1994) outlined a four-level model for evaluating the effectiveness of training. These evaluative variables and their measures will be discussed in chapter six.

- *Level 1: Reaction.* The basic level of reaction to instruction is an affective outcome. Learners react to instruction positively or negatively, and this is measured with user satisfaction measures.
- *Level 2: Learning.* The next level of result from instruction is both affective and cognitive. You can assess whether there has been an improvement in attitude towards the topic, and whether there is an improvement in knowledge and skill levels of the learner.
- *Level 3: Behavior.* Results at this level focus on the learner's behavioral changes on the job. Is the learner a safer operator of hazardous equipment? Has the learner improved accuracy in job performance tasks?
- *Level 4: Results.* Organizations trying to measure return on investment usually focus on measurable results that occur because of instruction, from the organization's perspective. Business results can be measured by assessing performance on assignments after training. Some organizational decision makers believe that "ROI" can and should be calculated before approving a major conversion project. It is more appropriate to do a benefit-cost analysis prior to conversion, and then use the evaluation process to conduct actual results based on learner performance after training. This book is not intended to provide the definitive economic model for completing an ROI analysis, but an outline of the process is provided. A detailed discussion of ROI as part of an evaluation process will be covered in chapter six.

There are four major steps in conducting an ROI analysis:

1. *Identifying the effects of training* (levels 1 through 4). This should include quantitative as well as qualitative effects.
2. *Converting effects to monetary values.* Direct conversion of quantitative effects, and indirect conversion of qualitative effects are developed.
3. *Calculating the costs of training initiatives.*
4. *Calculate the ROI.*

$$\% \text{ Return on investment (ROI)} = \frac{\text{Net program benefits}}{\text{Program costs}} \times 100$$

Chapter V

Multimedia Content Development

Instructional materials used in a traditional classroom setting can include text (books, handouts, articles), graphs, photos, films, and audio tapes. In the DL environment, these materials are digitized for delivery via a computer and/or a network.

This chapter presents topics related to multimedia content development for delivery in a DL environment. First, a discussion of file and format specifications for digital multimedia content is presented; second, levels of courseware complexity are discussed; third, steps in the courseware development process are described; and fourth, commercial off-the-shelf (COTS) tools for developing multimedia instructional content and computer managed instruction (CMI) are presented.

MULTIMEDIA CONTENT TYPES

Multimedia files are digitized and saved in different formats based on established and emerging standards. There is a tradeoff between file size and the resolution of the image or sound; there is another tradeoff between speed (time to download) and quality (fidelity) of the image or sound. What this means is that, in general, as sensory fidelity increases, the file sizes increase with a correspondent burden on speed and performance of the computer in displaying the image or sound.

Text

Basic elements of multimedia content are represented in text. Hypertext is a word or phrase that the user can click on to be linked to another document or segment of the document. As described in chapter two, hypertext can be used in multimedia documents for cross-referencing of information, for providing extended details about a word or concept and for navigating from a certain document to another document.

Graphics

There are two types of graphic images: bitmapped and object-oriented. Bitmapped images are composed of very tiny dots (called "pixels") arranged on a grid. The number of pixels in an image for screen graphics is measured in width times height of the image, e.g., 1024 x 768, 640 x 400, 800 x 600. For print graphics, pixels are measured as dots per inch (dpi), and common resolutions include 300 dpi, 600 dpi, and 9600 dpi. Bitmapped graphics are easy to manipulate with software tools that change the color or shade of each pixel. The range of colors represented by the pixels depends on how many bits are used to represent each pixel. Monochrome images require 1-bit image and can only represent two colors, black and white. A 4-bit image can represent 16 colors, 8-bits 256 colors, 16-bits 65,534 colors, and 24 bits 16.7 million colors.

Compression algorithms are applied to bitmapped files to reduce their size. Three types of compression algorithms are commonly used: RLE (run length encoding), LZ (Lempel-Ziv) and JPEG (joint photographic experts group). The most common file formats for bitmapped graphic images for the Web are Compuserv's GIF (*.gif) and JPG (*.jpg). GIF format can be represented by up to 8 bits per pixel (256 colors) and is best for drawn images, with transparency and animation possible. The advantage of GIF images is that all pixels are saved with the image, and there is no loss of pixels during compression. This means that the image can later be reconstructed back to its original fidelity. JPG files are 24 bits per pixel (true color) but lose information during compression and are best for photographic images. A new Internet standard for bitmapped images is PNG, which provides no loss during compression (like GIF), but provides high 24-bit color like JPG. There are several Commercial Off The Shelf (COTS) software tools that you can use to edit bitmapped images. Among them are Adobe PhotoShop® (http://www.adobe.com), Corel PhotoPaint® (http://www.corel.com), and Macromedia xRes® (http://www.macromedia.com/).

Object-oriented image files (also called vectored images) are different than bit-mapped images because they are composed of geometric shapes that can be selected, moved, layered, and manipulated while retaining their shape. Typical object shapes include ovals, circles, lines, and polygons. Typical manipulations include stretching, rotating and skewing. Curved lines are manipulated through "splines," which can be bent into different shapes. These curves have "anchor points" which can be pulled and moved through use of a mouse. Object-oriented graphics are not composed of pixels, so they appear very smooth, and are not dependent on the resolution of the image. Typical object-oriented formats include Postscript EPS (*.eps), AutoCAD (*.dxf), CorelDraw (*.cdr). COTS products used to create and edit object-oriented images include Adobe Illustrator® (http://www.adobe.com), CorelDRAW® (http://www.corel.com), Macromedia Freehand® (http://www.macromedia.com), and MetaCreations Fractal Expression® (http://www.metacreations.com.

Two-dimensional graphics (2D) give depth and perspective to flat images. Three-dimensional (3D) images offer the ability to place objects within a scene with photo realism. COTS products for 3D modeling include Template Graphic's 3Space Publisher® (http://www.tgs.com) for PCs and Specular's Infini-D® (http://www.zutroy.com/Infini-D/links.html) for Macintosh.

Animation

Two dimensional (2D) animations can also be bitmapped or object-oriented. Bitmapped animation is drawn, and the motion effect is created through the frames per second showing progressive movement. Full motion video requires 30 frames per second (FPS); a minimum of 10 fps is required to eliminate the "strobe" effects with animation. 2D animation tools include Macromedia Director® and Macromedia Flash® and GIF89a®. GIF89a is simple bitmapped animation and is handled natively by the browser. Macromedia Flash can be used to create object-oriented animations, allows for audio and simple interaction, and it runs with plug-ins such as Active X or Java applets. Macromedia Director can produce animations that move across the screen (called "sprite" animations), allows for audio and complex interaction, and runs with plug-ins; however this product usually requires that a multimedia developer create the animation.

Sound and Music Files

Sound is an important component of multimedia instruction—speech, sound effects and music all contribute to the richness of the learning environment. There are several techniques by which sound bites can be included in learning modules. The most common audio file formats used to record sounds are Microsoft's (http://www.microsoft.com/) Waveform (*.wav), NeXT/Sun Sparc's (*.au), RealAudio (http://www.real.com/) (*.ra), and Macintosh Audio Interchange File Format (*.aiff). MIDI (Musical Instrument Digital Interface) is a music file format. MIDI is a protocol for controlling electronic instruments such as synthesizers, and contains only instructions for the performance of sound, not audio data. MIDI can only be used to perform sounds that have already been programmed; it cannot be used to playback speeches. Sound libraries and archives provide sources for sound clips. As with video libraries below, be sure to read and understand the copyright and usage rules. You can create your own sound effects by recording your own sounds. Similar to the resolution of graphic images, sound fidelity varies depending on the sampling rates of the sound. Sampling rate refers to the frequency with which the sound is recorded—larger sampling rates produce better sound fidelity. The common sampling range is 8,000 Hz (samples per second) for 8-bit mono sound recorded at 8,000 per second through 44,100 Hz, 16-bit stereo sound recorded at 172,000 per second for CD quality sound. Similar to graphic files, audio files are compressed using compression algorithms. Software tools used to edit sound include Sound Forge (http://www.sonicfoundry.com/) and SoundEdit 16 (http://www.macromedia.com/).

Video Files

Video clips can be obtained through many sources. Video cards allow for capturing video from VCRs, camcorders, and other video cameras. CD-ROMs, the Internet and video libraries are sources for video clips. Video files can be very large; although systematic planning can reduce the file sizes by keeping the display area small, trying out different frame rates, maintaining as little color depth as possible, and keeping the associated sound track as small as possible.

LEVELS OF COURSEWARE COMPLEXITY

In chapter two, we discussed the concept of interactivity. DL courseware is categorized into three levels, based on the complexity of the design and the types of media formats used in the presentation. The levels are also roughly equivalent to the level of technical difficulty and time required to develop the content. Let's first review the concept of interactivity and compare it with course complexity and courseware levels.

Interactivity

Interactivity in chapter two was described in several ways: interactive properties of the communications channel; interactivity between instructor and learner; interactivity between learner and other learners; and finally, interactivity between the learner and the instructional content. For courses that are currently delivered in traditional classroom settings, the conversion analysis outlined in chapter four is based on an assessment of the level of interactivity between learner and instructor and between learner and other learners. There is a relationship between these two types of interactivity and the required interactivity between learner and instructional content if the course is converted. The reason for this is that the course content that was previously delivered live by an instructor is now being substituted by the DL medium, and the instructional content contained or represented using that medium.

There is a relationship between the interactivity of the learner with instructional content and the technical complexity of the courseware to be developed. In general, the more complex the instructional content, the more engagement is necessary for learners to achieve instructional objectives and learning retention. This higher level of engagement generally requires more complex use of multimedia, i.e., a higher level of courseware development. The relationship between learner-courseware interactivity and courseware development level is summarized below.

There are four levels of interactivity between the learner and the instructional content: 1) passive, 2) limited participation, 3) complex participation, and 4) real-time participation. This categorization includes learner-content, learner-learner, and learner-instructor types of interactivity. This is a finer-grained categorization than is presented in Figure 2.2 because it splits participation into limited and complex sub-categories.

Level of Interactivity and Associated Courseware Development Levels

As described in Table 5.1, there are four levels of interactivity, ranging from passive "page turning" to real-time participation. The table shows the increasing complexity of learning objectives (cognitive, psychomotor, or affective) that can be accomplished as interactivity levels rise. There is a comparable increase in the technical difficulty, cost, and complexity of courseware development as interactivity increases. Technical complexity in courseware development is described at three levels, and the relationship between these development levels and interactivity levels is shown in Table 5.2.

Level I: Text and Graphics

Courses that use only text and graphics range from e-mail based courses to Web-based courses. Web-based Level I courses can be augmented with on-line discussion forums, threaded discussions or bulletin boards. Using these communication technologies allows learners to interact with each other and with the instructor asynchronously and synchronously. Although Level I courseware does not have the interactivity of content as Level II courses or the multimedia components of Level III courses, they can still be engaging if they are well-designed.

Level I courses are inexpensive to build because they do not require multimedia authoring tools, audio and video editing tools, and they do not require a significant infrastructure to support delivery. A simple Web browser or access to email is sufficient to receive Level I training. If this infrastructure is already available, then the cost of Level I courseware will center on development of the content. Level I courses are appropriate if these some or all of these constraints apply to the organization, the instructors or the learners:

- The amount of course content is extensive.
- Bandwidth and infrastructure resources are scarce.
- The use of plug-ins is prohibited or not available for learner workstations.
- The course content must be updated very frequently.
- The learner population is widely dispersed with wide variations in infrastructure support and availability.
- Implementation costs must be kept to a minimum.

Level I courseware can be used in the combined DL situation or with technology insertion. In the combined DL case, the more dynamic, interactive, and communication-rich activities can be conducted with a live instructor. With technology insertion, the Level I course materials can be used for remediation or as a Web-enhanced course. Syllabi, lecture notes, practice exams, and other course materials can be posted on the Web, and learners can participate in

Table 5.1 Learner-Courseware Interactivity and Associated Learning Objectives

Student Interactivity With Courseware	Learning Objectives
Level 1: Passive • Learner interaction limited to advancing the presentation	**Cognitive** • Learning *facts* • Learning *rules* **Psychomotor** • *Perception* of normal/abnormal/emergency condition cues associated with performance of a procedure
Level 2: Limited Participation • Provides drill and practice • Provides feedback on learner responses • Can emulate simple psychomotor performance • Can emulate simple equipment operation in response to learner action • Computer evaluation of learner's cognitive performance	**Cognitive** • Learning *facts* • Learning *rules* • Learning step by step *procedures* **Psychomotor** • *Perception* of normal/abnormal/emergency condition cues associated with performance of a procedure • *Readiness* to take particular actions • *Guided response* in learning a complex physical skill **Affective** • *Receiving* normal/abnormal/emergency condition cues associated with performance of a procedure • *Responding* to cues

Table 5.1 (continued) Learner-Courseware Interactivity and Associated Learning Objectives

Student Interactivity With Courseware	Learning Objectives
Level 3: Complex Participation • Capable of complex branching paths based on student selection and responses • Can present or emulate complex procedures with explanations of equipment operation • Learner can participate in emulation of psychomotor performance and extensive branching capability • Capable of real-time simulation of performance in the operational setting • Computer evaluation of learner performance and intellectual skills • Computer evaluation of learner procedural performance includes time and errors scores	**Cognitive** • Learning step by step *procedures* • Learning to group and *discriminate* similar and dissimilar items • Learning to synthesize knowledge for *problem-solving* **Psychomotor** • *Perception* of normal/abnormal/emergency condition cues associated with performance of a procedure • *Readiness* to take particular actions • *Guided response* in learning a complex physical skill • Learning *mechanism* of performing complex physical skills • Learning *adaptation* to modify complex physical skills to accommodate a new situation • Learning *origination* to create new complex physical skills to accommodate a new situation • Learning to make *continuous movement*; compensate based on feedback **Affective** • *Receiving* normal/abnormal/emergency condition cues associated with performance of a procedure • *Responding* to cues • *Valuing* worth of quality of normal, abnormal, and emergency cues associated with performance of an operational procedure • Developing *competence* to make decisions using prioritized strategies and tactics in response to normal, abnormal, and emergency condition cues associated with performance of an operational procedure. • Learning *innovation* to make decisions
Level 4: Real-time Participation • Capable for real-time simulation of performance in the operational setting • Computer evaluation of learner performance and intellectual skills • Computer evaluation of learner procedural performance includes capability to generate time and error scores • Employs state-of-the-art technology for simulation and communication	**Cognitive** • Learning to group and *discriminate* similar and dissimilar items • Learning to synthesize knowledge for *problem-solving* Psychomotor • Learning *mechanism* of performing complex physical skills

Table 5.2 Interactivity and Courseware Development Levels

Interactivity Level	Courseware Development Level
1-2	I
2-3	II
4	III

threaded discussions and on-line forums. The course Web site can be used a repository where learners post their homework, projects, and papers. Useful links can be posted to external and internal Web sites. Many colleges and universities have fully developed Web sites and Intranet sites using Level I development to support the instructor and the learners in their courses.

Level I courseware is used for learning environments with limited participation. Cognitive objectives such as learning facts, rules, processes, and procedures can be accomplished at this level. Level I courseware does not generally allow to meet affective objectives because of the lack of richness of the media and the lower level of interactivity with the course content.

Level II: Interactive Text and Graphics

Level II courseware is distinguished by "interactive text." This is different than interactivity with the instructor or other learners described in Level I courseware using e-mail and on-line forums. Interactivity with the *content* means that the course has multiple branching alternatives, and learners are presented with different content and sequencing of content, depending on choices and decisions they make while progressing through this content. There are three methods by which interactive text can be built into courseware. The learner can use all three mechanisms together to search and view alternative navigation options and to take a particular branch through the content.

- *Table of Contents (TOC) or Index.* The TOC and index is the traditional navigation tool used in print materials. In CBT or WBT courses, the TOC or index is combined with hyperlinks to navigate through topics.
- *Hyperlinks.* Hyperlinks can be used in three ways. As described above, it is a navigational tool to topics listed in a TOC or index.

Second, course content can be "layered" or organized from the general to the detailed. Hyperlinks can provide more detailed or supplemental explanation of the course material. Third, from a cognitive standpoint, topics mentioned within the course content can be linked back to other sections within the course itself. This provides a psychological tool to reinforce relatedness of topics within the material itself. Thus, a learner might find that four times in the chapter, there were hyperlinks back to a particular subtopic. By noting these links, an association is built in the learner's mind linking the two related topics. This is a powerful learning tool that is not available to a learner reading straight text. Many instructors spend significant time in traditional lecture to build in these conceptual linkages in the minds of their students, but it is done in a one-way, receive-only mode by the learner. Computer-assisted associations between learner and instructional content are more powerfully made if the learner discovers these for himself through navigation through the course content.

- *Search Engine.* If there is a search capability in the courseware, the learner can locate associated or related links through specifying search criteria. The learner must enter a word or phrase and invoke the search engine. The search engine returns a list of hyperlinks, with a short description or the first two or three sentences of the document. The learner can select any of the hyperlinks to view the material. Each search engine works differently, but most use Boolean operators ("AND" "OR" "NOT") in conjunction with the key words specified in the search. Most search engines return the list of links based on a "relevance" criteria if multiple words are used in the search. For example, if I specify "electronic payment" "course administration" and "course management", the hyperlinks listed at the top will be the documents that meet all three criteria first. Thus, a topic about how universities can manage on-line courses using commercial products that provide Web-enabled course management systems for course administration, electronic payment and registration, etc, will score very high on the "relevance" criteria. Relevance criteria are based on meta-tags within the WBT or CBT document that identify key words about the document.

Interactive text also allows learners to become more engaged with the course content. There are many documented benefits of Level II courseware.

- *Tailored Instruction.* The course content is presented in a manner that is more personalized to the learner's preferences and thinking process. The learner can control the presentation of the content.
- *Increased Engagement.* This results in higher motivation and learning retention. The more engaged the learner is with the material, the higher the rate of retention.
- *Decreased Instructional Time.* Studies show that there is a direct correlation between level of engagement by the learner and the time it takes to master the material.

Level II courseware allows for the practice of skills using learned facts and processes, emulation of analytical situations and what the learner's appropriate response(s) should be. It also enables learners to demonstrate that affective learning objectives have been met through appropriate responses to the course content by demonstrating that certain values have been learned and applied to situations requiring the application of human judgment. For example, a scenario with multiple "what if" threads or outcomes could be tied to instructional material about ethical guidelines that require the learner to identify and select the appropriate situational behaviors associated with compliance with company policies.

Level III: Interactive Multimedia

Level III courseware is the most expensive, complex, and fully interactive type of DL instruction. Interactive text is combined with video, sound, animation and high-resolution graphics to provide learners with a rich learning environment that can engage all their senses (except smell). Some characteristics of Level III courseware include:

- Complex branching paths based on learner selection and responses.
- Complex procedures can be emulated.
- Psychomotor actions that require cognitive skills and judgement can be simulated for an operational setting.
- The courseware is able to track and evaluate all aspects of the learner's performance.

- In addition to feedback on performance, the courseware can present a sequence of remedial content material or exercises to remediate gaps in learning.
- Cognitive objectives involving the learner's ability to discriminate, solve complex problems and demonstrate effective judgement can be accomplished.
- The courseware can engage the learner at the affective level in combination with cognitive objectives, so that the learner's performance can be linked to successful internalization of values, mental preparedness, customer-orientation, leadership and other important "soft" skills.

Since level III courseware includes large multimedia files (audio, video, animation, and many branching text files), technical infrastructure becomes an issue in the delivery of level III courses. WBT courses over the Internet are especially problematic due to the long download times. There are technologies, such as Macromedia's Shockwave®, that can help bring WBT training to the desktop over the Internet.

Shockwave® is a technology that breaks down a large multimedia application into small chunks with compression. The program can then be downloaded in small increments and run without having to wait until the entire program downloads. The application runs at the server end but does require a plug-in installed at the user's workstation. Shockwave can be used to convert multimedia courses developed in Authorware by using a tool called Afterburner. A "shocked" application will have one or more "segment" files and one "map" file. The segments are the small compressed files that make up the application, and the map file contains location and instructions to start streaming the segments. Shockwave® is platform independent, meaning that the course can be delivered to the learner's workstation regardless of type of computer, as long as he or she has an appropriate plug-in installed (which are specific to his or her computer platform). Table 5.3 provides details of features of DL courseware by level.

STEPS IN THE DEVELOPMENT PROCESS

The development process is a major phase of the ADDIE lifecycle. Development is, in fact, what most people think of when they talk about course conversion. As a major phase in the ADDIE cycle, it is composed of several important steps.

Table 5.3 Level of Courseware by Supported Features

Feature	Level I	Level II	Level III
On screen text	Yes	Yes	Yes
4-bit (16-colors) and lower	Yes	Yes	Yes
Low-end (simple) graphics	Yes	Yes	Yes
Low-end (simple) animations	Yes	Yes	Yes
8-bit (256-colors) and lowerNo	Yes	Yes	
Mid-range graphics	No	Yes	Yes
Mid-range animations	No	Yes	Yes
Control panels and multi-level navigational menus	No	Yes	Yes
User text entry and manipulation	No	Yes	Yes
8-bit audio (FM quality)	No	Yes	Yes
Audio track (voice only)	No	Yes	Yes
Streaming audio/video technology	No	Yes	Yes
Local user record	No	Yes	Yes
Half-motion (15 fps) video segments with audio	No	Yes	Yes
Periodic review questions	No	Yes	Yes
Audio track (voice / background music)	No	No	Yes
High-end (complex) graphics (photographic quality)	No	No	Yes
High-end (complex) animations (virtual reality simulations & 3D models)	No	No	Yes
16-bit (64,000-colors) and lower	No	No	Yes
16-bit audio (CD quality)	No	No	Yes
Full-motion (30 fps) video segments with audio	No	No	Yes
User registration, testing, and record keeping (Course Management System)	No	No	Yes
1- or 2-way desktop videoconferencing	No	No	Yes
E-mail capability	No	No	Yes
Voice recognition technology	No	No	Yes
Intelligent assistant (Agent)	No	No	Yes

Planning the Development Process

There are four major steps in a DL conversion process. The first step is to create a project plan that identifies each phase of the development cycle, outputs of that phase, who is responsible for the inputs and outputs of that phase, the estimated time of completion, and the procedures required to get a review and approval at each step. The project plan can be created using word processing, spreadsheet, or project management tools. A good place to start is the document used to estimate the project cost described in the last chapter.

Outline of the development process

It is useful from a strategic, organizational and business perspective to outline the entire development process. This document, which can be a brief text document, a spreadsheet or project management file, identifies all major tasks, roles and responsibilities through the entire development process.

Develop quality control procedures

At each step in the development process outlined above, ask the question, "What would be my worst nightmare?" or "What things could go wrong at this stage?" After identifying processes that could go wrong, think of ways to measure and assess performance of that process, and what indicators would help keep that project on track in the right direction. For example, during the instructional design process, subject matter experts (SMEs) work with instructional systems designers (ISDs) to lay out a storyboard design for the courseware. The story board shows the content, flow, and hierarchy of information and decision flows that the learner would work through. What if the SMEs do not know what the learning objectives were as they work with ISDs? The result might be a poorly designed course, or a well

Figure 5.1 Development Process

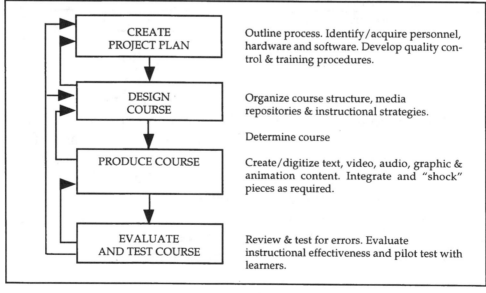

designed course that does not help the learner to achieve his or her learning objectives. An example of a quality control procedure would be to have both the subject matter expert and the instructional systems designer review detailed documentation on learning objectives of each unit before the storyboarding process begins.

Determine hardware, software, and media requirements

A useful inventory form for your current capabilities is provided in Appendix C. Note that the survey is completed from two perspectives—the learner's infrastructure and the instructor/organization. Infrastructure is available as a "lowest common denominator" phenomena because the learner's workstation capabilities must match those of the providing organization. For example, if the organization's modem pool allows for 56 KBPS, but the learner's modem is only 28.8 KBPS, the transfer of data between the learner's workstation and the delivery organization would occur at a maximum of 28.8 KBPS only. Likewise, even if the learner subscribed to ISDN service, if the delivery organization did not provide ISDN connectivity to its dialup clients, the learner would not be able to connect using that ISDN service.

Identify staffing requirements

As discussed in chapter four, the organization must decide whether to use in-house support, freelance support, or contractor support. Every conversion project requires a diverse set of technical, management, business, and instructional design skills. A successful conversion project requires the right mix and match of skills.

Determine if training is required

Training may be required when using in-house staff. This may include technology refreshment courses or advanced technology courses to get "up to speed" with the most recent learning technologies.

Make staff assignments

Specialization of skills on a project is often a luxury. Even the largest projects require personnel to be multi-talented in at least two areas. For example, it might be expected that an HTML programmer also know a little about programming in CGI, Javascript, Java, or other scripting language. That person may also need to know something about multimedia editing (audio and video) for the project. A common error on projects (often in hindsight) is to only focus on technical positions required for a conversion effort. Don't forget that project managers, economic and business analysts, and other "non-technical" personnel are key requirements for success of the project.

Hire outside support if necessary

The saying about doctors and lawyers, "the doctor/lawyer who treats himself has a fool for a client" applies to conversion projects as well. The full range of personnel skills required for a successful course implementation should be considered, and outside support should be hired if necessary. A common mistake is to assume that one can expect in-house personnel to pick up and learn a new technology/language/skill for the project. They may take a few courses and learn the new skill, but if the job responsibility requires technical leadership and experience, then the project risk is increased because the person may not know "what they don't know." Once the project team is put in place, the next step is to begin designing the course.

Designing the Course

The task of designing the course is often the most exciting and creative part of the project. It is a structured and methodological step, yet it allows for tremendous creativity in the process.

Lay out the organization and structure of the course to be developed

The course should be broken down into instructional units or modules, as discussed in chapter four. The units/modules should be organized around the general theme of the course as well as the learning objectives of each unit.

Develop instructional strategies

Instructional design strategies include tutorial, scenario exploration, simulation, game, and embedded questions. The "art" of instructional design comes into play in the consideration and choice of appropriate and engaging strategies. Experienced instructional designers work together with subject matter experts to determine which instructional strategies can best achieve the learning objectives of the module.

Define components of the lessons or instructional units to be developed

Each learning module could be composed of text files, digitized video or audio clips or graphics. The package of one instructional unit of DL delivery is like a suitcase packed for travel. The unit (suitcase) is packed with several items such as toothbrush, comb, pants, socks, and shirts.

Determine which file formats you will use

Continuing with the suitcase analogy, this is like deciding that it will be brand X toothbrush, brand Y toothpaste, brand Z pants, etc. Multimedia files have different formats, as discussed earlier in this chapter.

Organize and structure your media repositories

The number of files for any learning module can be very large. The different media formats should have structured folders or directories for storage. For example, all image files could be stored in a directory called /images. Within the /image directory, there could be multiple sub-directories for types of images, such as /images/balls, /images/ arrows, /images/icons. There could be a similar repository structure for sound or video files.

Design the screens

The user interface screens should be designed with a clean, consistent interface. There should be navigation buttons/icons to get back to all previous screens, including the top level page.

Develop storyboards showing sequence and high level content, and branching

All options taken by the learner should be mapped out in the storyboard. These branching screens can be evaluated for their effectiveness in providing feedback on both correct and incorrect decision options. Flowcharts are effective methods by which to develop linear, tree, cluster, and star-shaped decision structures.

Producing the Course

After the storyboards are completed, course production begins. This is the authoring or programming phase of course conversion. The difficulty, cost, and time required to complete this step depends on the complexity of the course (level 1, 2, or 3). The producer may need to develop audio and video segments, and text-based content. If the course is an existing one, then many materials (text files and graphics) can be converted for DL use. Different production tasks can occur at the same time, and they are all brought together with an authoring tool.

Producing/digitizing video content

Video segments can be digitized (recorded on a computer) using a special card that converts analog video signals into a digital value for each pixel. During conversion, any analog image from a camera, videodisc or broadcast TV can be used as input for digital conversion. Digitized video files are extremely large (for example, one second of a full motion video at 30 frames per second can be almost 20 MB in size).

Producing/digitizing audio content

Analog voice signals can be digitally recorded with a microphone on a PC or writeable CD-ROM. Audio clips can also be taken from existing recorded music, sound effects, voice narratives, or can be purchased from third party vendors.

Creating graphic content

Graphics software can be used to design and create graphic images, or existing images can be imported as a graphic file. If you have a hard copy of an image, it can be scanned into digital format and saved as a graphics file for use in the program.

Producing animation

If graphics are put into motion, they are animated. They are time consuming to develop, so they should be used when the animation adds significant interest level to the material or engages the learner. An example of animated graphics would be an animated character that provides suggestions for obtaining help and guides the learner through the course content.

Authoring/programming

At this step, the text, audio, graphics, video, and sound files are integrated together, based on the storyboard, flowcharts, and outline of the course. The features and functionality of several authoring tools are described later in this chapter.

Developing "shocked" pieces for delivery over the Internet

A product like Macromedia's Shockwave can be used to process the large files for courseware delivery into smaller, segmented files that can be downloaded and activated on the learner's workstation.

As the courseware is produced, evaluation and testing procedures should be concurrently conducted, as outlined below. A more detailed discussion of overall evaluation is presented in chapter six.

Evaluation and Testing

Courseware development and production is an iterative process. One way to combine continual evaluation and testing with courseware development and production is to use a prototype development approach and to pilot test the result with actual learners.

Review for content errors

Subject matter experts are the best reviewers of courseware for content accuracy, clarity and understandability. Sometimes during conversion of existing course content, text-based information is condensed and/or broken down into smaller delivery segments and hyperlinked as part of the design. A SME should review the new non-linear design of content presentation to ensure that the accuracy of the information is preserved.

Evaluate for instructional effectiveness

An instructional systems designer and the course manager are the best people to continually assess the developing product for instructional effectiveness. They will be assessing whether the design, layout, and storyboard flow as it is programmed achieves the learning objectives of each module, whether the appropriate emphasis is being placed on concepts as it is transformed into multimedia formats.

Test for technical errors

The programmers will work with the SMEs and ISDs during prototype development to test the system for errors. Examples of technical errors would be links that do not work, incorrect flow through the lessons, or inconsistent navigation.

Pilot test with learners

Prototype development can be combined with pilot testing of the product with actual learners. As discussed in the last chapter, a decision should be made on whom the sample population of learners should be—their level of technology competence, their learning needs, their attitude towards DL and instructional technologies, their availability, and their ability to detect errors and make useful suggestions for improvement.

FEATURES AND FUNCTIONS OF TOOLS FOR DEVELOPING MULTIMEDIA INSTRUCTIONAL CONTENT AND COMPUTER MANAGED INSTRUCTION

This section describes the features and functionality of seven commercial off-the-shelf (COTS) products: **Learning Space**, **WebCT**, **TopClass**, **Toolbook**, **Web Course in a Box** and two products by Blackboard: **CourseInfo** and **Campus**.

Features and Functions of COTS Products

Functionality of these development products should be examined from four key perspectives: 1) the learner, 2) the instructor, 3) the technical administrator, and 4) the learning organization. The comments contained here are not exhaustive but are intended to provide information on useful features, functions and tools that serve each of the four key stakeholder categories.

Supporting the Learner

Farance and Tonkel (1998, p.47) discuss the "human centered features" of the learner-environment interaction. They argue that human learners have characteristics that must be considered when designing systems for the learner.

- "Humans receive information via sensory input and/or physical interactions."
- "Human aren't reliable receivers of information."
- "Humans are diverse and are unpredictable receivers of information."
- "Human are nomadic—they learn at different places and learn differently over time."
- "Humans are self-aware and can give advice on themselves."
- "A single human can play several roles; several humans can play a single role."
- "Several learning experiences may be occurring simultaneously."

Given these characteristics of human learners, features/tools of the products required to support the learner include Web browsing, asynchronous and synchronous sharing and learner tools (Landon, 1998). A detailed glossary of the terms used in this section is provided in Appendix B.

Web Browsing. Since the early 1990's, the Web browser has become the universal interface to information content on the Internet. Most COTS products take advantage of this easy-to-use interface and use either a browser (e.g., Netscape, Internet Explorer) or a browser-like interface for navigation though the course. For new or inexperienced computer users, the browser interface is intuitive and easy to learn.

- *Accessibility.* Access for persons with disabilities by providing for a universal text version that does not rely solely on frames, tables, or images.
- *Bookmarks.* Bookmarks identify Internet locations or "URLs". The feature allows the learner to control the creation, display, management and updating of bookmarks.
- *Multimedia Support.* Support for images, audio, video and VRML files within the course.
- *Security.* Support for secure transactions on the Web and ability to verify the security of downloaded code.

Asynchronous Sharing. Learners need to interact with other learners and with the instructor, sometimes asynchronously and sometimes synchronously. The advantage of asynchronous communication tools is that information can be posted or shared without the presence of the recipient. Learners and the instructor can send and receive messages at their own pace and convenience through e-mail, BBS (Bulletin Board Service) file exchange, or newsgroups.

Synchronous Sharing. During certain learning activities synchronous communication tools are required. These include group problem solving, group discussions, or other communication activity where the synergy of multiple participants is required to achieve learning. Synchronous sharing allows students and/or the instructor to participate in real-time in a virtual "place" where each participant can collaborate in text-based messages (using chat or whiteboards), or share control of the mouse (application sharing). Other synchronous sharing can be accomplished with Virtual Spaces (MUDs, MOOs or virtual meeting rooms), Group Browsing (group tours of Web sites with a shared browser window, some interaction capability between the members of the group and the tour leader), Teleconferencing, or Videoconferencing.

Learner Tools. In traditional classroom environments the instructor is the only one who provides feedback on the learner's progress. DL environments offer an additional benefit by providing automated tools that help learners to assess their own learning and progress in their lessons. These tools can help build motivation and engagement of the learner and can provide skill building support.

- *Self-assessment Capability.* Capability to do practice quizzes and other performance assessment using tools that may or may not be scored online.
- *Progress Tracking.* Learner's ability to check scores on assignments and tests.
- *Motivation Building.* Self-help tools and other facilities that provide direct encouragement to overcome difficulties that impede or impair learner performance.
- *Study Skill Building.* Capability to support effective study practices, which can range from simple review tools to mini-courses on "how to study."

Supporting the Instructor
Pedagogical responsibilities of the instructor, regardless of whether

it is for traditional classroom learning or a DL environment, include course/curriculum design and management, instructional design and development, evaluating and assessing learner performance, marking and tracking of learner grades, interacting and giving feedback to learners, and managing the overall learning environment within the course. The following features and tools of COTS products would provide support for the instructor in DL courseware.

Course Tools. The features and functions required to support instructors in managing their courses include tools that facilitate course planning, managing, and revising.

- *Course Planning.* Tools that enable at least initial course layout and or structuring.
- *Course Managing.* Capability for instructors to collect information from or about learners related to their progress in the course and to permit/deny access to course resources.
- *Rapid Course Revising.* The ability to change the structure of the course and its assignments, exams, etc. with relative ease.
- *Course Monitoring.* Capability to provide information about the usage of course resources by individual learners and groups of learners.

Lesson Tools. Instructors who manage their own DL courses need tools that help them maintain course content and develop testing materials.

- *Instructional Design.* Tools that help instructors create learning sequences, such as storyboarding.
- *Presentation.* Facilities for formatting, displaying, or showing course material over the Web.
- *Testing.* Tools that support the development of quizzes, tests, exams, and other assignments.

Data Tools. Instructor tools to support the management and manipulation of learner data provide functionality for grading online and tracking learner performance.

- *Marking Online.* Capability to mark learner-generated material while online.

- *Managing Records*. Facilities for organizing and keeping track of course-related information.
- *Analyzing and Tracking*. Capability to perform statistical analysis of learner-related data; the ability to display the progress of individual learners in the course structure.

Resource Tools. Some of these tools include:
- *Building Knowledge*. Capability to accumulate and share the knowledge gained by individual instructors through their experience with distance education. Examples range from simple Q&A files to extensive data warehouses of tips, workarounds and class exercises.
- *Team Building*. Collaborative facilities and features that allow individuals to build synergy through their interaction; to get to know each other and work more effectively together.
- *Building Motivation*. Facilities for self-help (and possibly other help such as a "buddy system") to provide encouragement and enhance morale.

Supporting the Technical Administrator

The technical administrators perform the day-to-day operational maintenance of a DL environment. For technical efficiency, security, and organizational reasons, it a preferable to manage DL courses at the enterprise level. This becomes a necessity as the number of DL courses increases within and across curricula. The following features and tool sets would be required to perform technical support functions effectively.

Installation Tools. Technical administrators are responsible for installing the products on the server side; users (course managers, instructors, learners) are usually responsible for installing the products on the user's workstation.

- *Server*. Server-side utility software may be included to facilitate the installation process, including on-line troubleshooting assistance, diagnostics, and reporting statistics.
- *Client*. The learner's workstation installation usually includes browser software, plug-ins, e-mail packages and other software. A good COTS package would simplify the process and facilitate the automatic installation of these applications.

System Tools. Systems administrators are also usually responsible for security management of the system and must add and delete authorized users, create user groups, set and monitor access privileges for users.

- *Authorization Tools.* Tools that assign access and other privileges to specific users or user groups.
- *Security Tools.* Utility software tools to configure security options, features, and functions within the operating environment of the product.
- *Resource Monitoring.* Tools to prevent unauthorized access and/ or modification of data. Includes a wide range of approaches and methods.
- *Remote Access Tools.* Software functions that allow a systems administrator to log on with supervisory privileges from any workstation, or dialing in from a remote location.
- *Crash Recovery Tools.* System, application, and data recovery functions provided by the software.

Help Desk Tools. All users of the system will require some technical support. Help Desk tools are software features that simulate a traditional telephone call-in center.

- *Learner support tools.* Tools that support learners include tutorials on how to get started as a new student in an enrolled course; features that allow learners to request help from a support staff (usually this is accomplished with e-mail links); frequently asked questions and answers; and links to technical information. The ability for learners to provide feedback to Help Desk support personnel is an important way to continually improve services.
- *Instructor support tools.* Instructors need occasional support on how to use features and functions of the different utilities; there may be a shared collaborative area ("teachers' lounge") where instructors can provide useful tips to each other.

Technical Infrastructure Considerations

The functions and features of COTS products described above require an infrastructure of hardware and software. The minimum requirements vary among products, and these should be evaluated against the capabilities of your existing and planned infrastructure.

The Infrastructure Survey (Appendix C) is a useful tool to document the functions and capabilities of your existing infrastructure.

Server Platform. Each COTS product will specify the minimum technical requirements for the server hardware and operating system.

- *RAM.* Random access memory, specified in MB (megabytes). Products specify the minimum RAM required of the server.
- *Disk Space.* The amount of hard disk storage space required for the program to operate.
- *Windows NT 4.0.* Microsoft Windows NT version 4.0 server operating system software (version 5.0 was recently renamed Windows 2000).
- *Apple Server.* An Internet server running the Apple Computer Operating System.
- *UNIX Server.* Unix operating system software, sometimes customized to a specific hardware vendor, i.e. Solaris for Sun Servers.

Client Platform. Two levels of client performs could be required.
- *Minimum Level.* Lowest level of browser that can be used with the application, e.g., Netscape 2.0, 3.0, 4.0, Internet Explorer 2.0, 3.0.
- *Target Level.* Level of browser that was intended to work best with the application, e.g., Netscape 4.05 or Internet Explorer 4.0.

Pricing. Several costs must be considered.
- *Startup Cost.* The initial cost of acquiring the application and getting it running locally.
- *Ongoing Cost.* The continuing year to year application costs for licensing, service contracts, beyond the start-up cost.
- *Technical Support.* The cost of support for technical administrators that is provided from the application vendor.

Limitations. The COTS packages may have limitations in the way the software may be used, from a technical capability standpoint, or a pricing standpoint.

- *Number of Courses.* Products may have limits on the number of courses that can be accommodated by the software capacities or the license.

- *Number of Learners*. There may be limits on the number of learners that can be enrolled in a course using course management systems or by terms of the license.
- *Number of Connections*. There may be limits on the number of simultaneous Internet connections to a course Web site by capacity of the software or terms of the license.
- *Number of Instructors*. There may be limits of the number of instructors that can be supported by capacity of the software or terms of the license.
- *Other Limitations*. Check the product literature for any other limitations of the products.

Other Considerations. Some additional considerations are outlined here.

- *Options*. Products usually contain one or more features of the application that are not necessary, but perhaps desirable add-ons to the basic package.
- *Exit Considerations*. These are factors that are only important when changing from one application to another, these often involve translating data from a proprietary format to a common format so that the new application can read the data from the old application.
- *IMS Project Participant*. The IMS (Instructional Management System) project is an open consortium of industry and education members who are developing a more sophisticated framework for distributed computer-based learning. They are developing a set of specifications and prototype software for facilitating the growth and viability of distributed learning on the Internet. The IMS is focusing on the development of standards for learning objects. Many vendors are participants in this project and have a vested interest in the development of industry standards for distributed learning.

Supporting the Learning Organization
Over the past decade, much effort has been devoted to the modernization of computing systems in institutions of higher learn-

ing—in particular, to automate or upgrade payroll systems, human resource systems and admissions processes. However, not much progress has been made to upgrade the computing systems that serve the core business of those institutions —i.e., systems that support the instructional staff and the students. Course Management Systems (CMS) are emerging as a group of tools and applications that will provide integrated tools for the creation and management of an on-line learning environment.

In order to support the learning environment at the enterprise level, organizations must implement open architectures, and standards-based network technologies. There must be a strategy and plan to create, index, store, and retrieve reusable learning content. There should also be a strong collaborative relationship among private industry, the training and education community and the federal government for the specification of user requirements and its corresponding COTS product development.

The U.S. Department of Defense, one of the largest user communities of education and training in the world, has defined its broad general requirements for the development of advanced distributed learning environments.

The following capabilities are required to support the learning organization.

- *Accessibility* from any location, remote or local.
- *Interoperability* between all advanced distributed learning instructional platforms, media, and tools.
- *Durability* to withstand base technology changes without significant recoding or redesign.
- *Reusability* between applications, platforms, and tools.
- *Cost Effectiveness* to provide significant increases in learning and readiness per net increment in time or cost.

To support the learning organization, COTS products must commit and provide three categories of products/services.

Standards-Based Interoperable Platforms. Standards for learning systems have not fully emerged at this time, but there are "de facto" standards being developed by vendors at the forefront of instructional technology applications. There are standards committees, such as the

IEEE Learning Technology Standards Committee. As emerging standards become published, vendors will be able to develop standards-based products that will be interoperable across different platforms and can be engineered for seamless integration with other COTS products.

Reusable Learning Content. When courses within a curriculum are developed, planning should be done to identify, tag, and organize learning modules, multimedia files, and text that may be reusable in other courses. Learning object modules and their associated files must be indexed and stored in a database so that it can be retrieved and used in other courses. In the future, COTS development tools will include the capability to interface with learning object databases.

Digital Knowledge Repositories. Digital libraries containing knowledge-related products for learning should be established early in the development lifecycle for large courseware conversions.

SELECTED COURSEWARE DEVELOPMENT AND COURSE MANAGEMENT SYSTEMS TOOLS

In this section, we provide information on functions and features of seven COTS products. Check their Web sites for the most current and planned features, and for more details.

LearningSpace (http://www.lotus.com/home.nsf/tabs/ learnspace)

Lotus LearningSpace provides tools for media-rich, collaborative learning and knowledge management. Five collaborative learning modules are combined to deliver an integrated environment that supports team-based and instructor-facilitated learning.

Learner Tools

LearningSpace supports all multimedia file formats, which can be attached to LearningSpace documents. Security is provided at several levels, from user authentication for course access to participation in private/public discussions and work projects. E-mail is used for notification of learner assignments, receipt of instructor assessments, alerts to changes/additions to course schedules, and for private discussions outside of the LearningSpace CourseRoom. Files are deposited and exchanged through MediaCenter, which serves as the course repository. The CourseRoom serves as the "newsgroup" function in LearningSpace.

The Schedule facility is a structuring mechanism for course assignments. Learners are able to navigate through course learning objectives, check deadlines for assignments, and access course syllabi.

The Profiles facility is a repository of learner-created "home pages." Learners can enter and update phone and address information, create links to their favorite Web sites, and add a photo to their personal profile. Learners also have an individual portfolio to store their assessments and assignments.

Instructor Tools

Course planning support is provided through a hierarchical outline facility and the use of course templates. The Schedule facility is the roadmap for the course—it links participants to assignments, quizzes, surveys, and self-assignments. Using the Schedule facility, instructors can customize welcome pages, use a variety of graphical icons to categorize assignments, enable/disable CourseRoom discussion buttons, and preserve links to MediaCenter and CourseRoom when copying courses. Schedule accommodates self-paced or team-based learning environments.

The MediaCenter is a knowledge base and reference tool for course-related content. The instructor can use MediaCenter to incorporate multimedia files, graphics, and Web links into courses without any knowledge of HTML.

The CourseRoom facility is an interactive environment for learner/teams, learner/peers, and learner/instructor collaboration. The facility allows for private learner-to-learner and learner-to-instructor discussions, and provides the instructor with grading tools.

The Assessment Manager tool allows instructors to do learner evaluations and provides learners with feedback on their performance. The testing facility allows for randomized questions; the ability to track and limit how many assessments the student can take. Questions can be categorized for ease in creating tests, and questions can be imported from test banks. The instructor can return corrected assignments to the learners' portfolios. There is a "quick grade" feature that allows for auto-grading and the recording of assessments.

Technical/Administrative Tools

There are tools that allow for customizing the look and feel of

LearningSpace. Custom functions and modules can be built. There are also tools that manage the process of learner enrollment and access. The CoursePack feature allows for the management and distribution of course content, move and copy courses.

Synchronous communication facilities are available with LearningSpace with the companion product called DataBeam Learning Server. Learning Server 2.0 provides the capability for chat, whiteboard, application sharing, group browsing, teleconferencing, and desktop videoconferencing.

Technical Information

LearningSpace version 2.5 requires Domino 4.5x or 4.6x server. Users access LearningSpace through a Netscape 3.5 or higher browser or Internet Explorer 4.x or higher. LearningSpace can also be accessed from Lotus Notes 4.51+ client. Supported platforms include Microsoft NT, IBM OS/2, IBM AIX, IBM 390, HP-UX, and Sun Solaris. LearningSpace can be purchased through Lotus authorized resellers (http://www.lotus.com) or the IBM Global Campus (http://www.ibm.com).

WebCT (http://homebrew1.cs.ubc.ca/webct/)

WebCT provides a number of learner, instructor and technical tools that support a multimedia learning environment.

Learner Tools

WebCT tracks each learner's last visited page of course content, and returns the learner to that page on the next visit. Multimedia files can be attached to any page of content. The files can be categorized and presented in a table format for viewing by the learner. Access to WebCT courses is managed through username and password. Course designers can provide learners the ability to create their own accounts. E-mail functions are integrated with learner tracking and grade maintenance tools, so that learners with a particular grade or participation characteristics can be sent group e-mail. There is an asynchronous bulletin board capability that can support multiple forums and is threaded and searchable. The only synchronous function supported on the same server is on-line chat. There is self-assessment support for quizzes through automatic grading, and progress tracking statistics that can be optionally released to the learner. Learners can build their own home pages for the course without any knowledge of HTML. Building study skills can be accomplished through on-line note taking, the ability of learners to generate study guides of topics selected by themselves, and ability to annotate content.

Instructor Tools

Instructors can use a number of tools to facilitate the design and construction of instructional content. Standard templates are provided for course outlines, assignments, and reading lists.

Group/course scheduling can be done using a calendar tool. Course revisions are easily accomplished online within WebCT. Progress statistics can be tracked from a learner perspective (access dates/times, frequency, conferencing tool usage) and also from a content perspective (number of accesses to each content page; average time spent on each page). Statistics are also provided for on-line quizzes (who is taking them, how learners are performing on the quizzes), and for system resources (course numbers, sizes, creation/modification dates).

Instructors use a learner records management feature to add student records, query records using searchable characteristics and can add arbitrary content categories to learner records (e.g., section number, attendance, comments).

At the instructor's discretion, learners can post comments/annotations within presentation areas on a page. Learners can be manually or automatically assigned into teams, with private conference areas for each group/team.

Technical/Administrative Tools

Server installation tools are available through a technical support arrangement. All courses are access controlled. The administrative interface is Web-based and provides information about resource usage (disk usage, number of students). On-line support for learners is provided for the conferencing feature and e-mail. Instructors are supported with context sensitive online help, as well as an online tutorial.

Technical Information

The WebCT server requires 32 MB of RAM and 10Mb for the system plus 2Mb per course and 30-70Kb per student. The server can run on Windows NT and Unix platforms. Learners only require a Web browser for access.

TopClass Server (http://www.wbtsystems.com/)

WBT Systems developed *TopClass* in 1995. It is an integrated course content and class management system. The product is designed to operate in a Web-based environment over the Internet/intranet and cannot operate in an off-line mode.

Learner Tools

TopClass is universally accessible through any Web browser, and is capable of using all multimedia file types. Its navigation toolbar has context sensitive buttons at the bottom. Individual access privileges are verified and managed for every request. The product provides several asynchronous collaboration tools, including a context aware messaging system, discussion list facility for multi-level bulletin boards, moderated discussions, threaded discussions, and file attachments. Instructors can use the Class Announcements facility to post general messages to all learners. *TopClass* provides learners with feedback on course materials they have reviewed, new material that has been assigned, and new messages in ongoing discussions that they are participating in. Learners see only material, assignments, and discussions that they are enrolled in.

Instructor Tools

TopClass provides mechanisms for authoring, maintaining, and distributing course content. A course outlining tool is provided, which can be used from any standard Web browser. No knowledge of HTML is required to build course content. Courses are easy to modify, and sections can be added, removed, or reordered, and are composed into hierarchical Units of Learning Material (ULM) modules. A ULM is a small unit of learning, which can be chunked into a learning module. ULM modules can be packed and transported as an entire course. All locally referenced files, including images, Shockwave, Java, or QuickTime files are copied into the Plug 'n' Play file, and can be transported to another *TopClass* server on any platform. ULM modules can also be used to create customized courses using selected modules from other lessons, courses, and curricula. ULM is central to the concept of reusability. This would allow organizations to buy third-party ULM courseware content and integrate it with locally developed ULMs.

TopClass provides auto-testing functionality, which is of value to the learner and the instructor. Instructors can create tests online (for grading by the server or manually by the instructor). The server can be configured to take actions based on learner performance on a test, such as assigning additional course material or notifying the instructor if the learner scores above or below instructor-defined thresholds.

Technical/Administrative Tools

Learners and instructors are grouped into "classes," but they can participate in more than one class. Learners are permitted to access and view material, assignments, and discussion groups for the classes they are enrolled in. Each class is associated with a default set of course material, which can be tailored, updated, or removed.

Technical Information

The *TopClass* server contains an object-oriented database that stores all information on users, content, and classes. The use of object-embedded information stores, as opposed to a relational database engine, provides flexibility, dynamism, and extensibility in this Web-based integrated environment. The *TopClass* server architecture is cross-platform. That is, database files created and used on one server (e.g., Windows NT) can be transferred to another *TopClass* server (e.g., Unix Solaris) without any conversion. *TopClass* is purchased by annual subscription. There is a free evaluation version.

Asymmetrix Toolbook (http://www.asymetrix.com/)

Toolbook is one of several integrated software products provided by Asymmetrix to support multimedia Web-based training and virtual learning environments.

Learner Tools

Bookmarks are supported to allow learners to resume where they left off. Multimedia files and security is not supported. E-mail use is supported without bulletin board or file exchange capability. Toolbook's Librarian provides synchronous communication via on-line discussion groups, whiteboard facilities, group browsing, and teleconferencing. It allows for installation of third-party software

(DataBeam's Learning Server®, Microsoft's NetMeeting®). Toolbook allows for progress tracking but does not provide learner self-assessment capability, or motivation and study skill building features.

Instructor Tools

Course planning tools are not provided, but the instructor can assign roles and lessons, set conditions, manage course content, and assign collaborative assignments to learners. Rapid course revising is possible through the incorporation of 3rd party content using Open Library Exchange. Course monitoring is supported with a database.

Toolbook provides many courseware authoring tools—templates, wizards, preprogrammed Catalog objects using the OpenScript programming language. Video files can be captured and edited using the Digital Video Producer and Digital Video Recorder. All multimedia file formats are supported.

On-line learner records management is not supported, and tests cannot be graded online. The product does not have tools that support building knowledge, team building or building motivation.

Technical/Administrative Tools

DataBeam's Learning Server can be integrated with Librarian to add synchronous communication facilities. No system tools are provided for authorizing users, security, resource monitoring, remote access, and crash recovery. There are no Help Desk tools supported.

Technical Information

Toolbook requires 32 MB of RAM (64 Mb recommended) and 15 MB of hard disk space. Windows NT and Unix servers are supported. SQL server is required to run Librarian.

Web Course in a Box (http://www.madduck.com/index.html)

MadDuck Technologies, a Virginia-based learning technologies company, developed Web Course in a Box.

Learner Tools

Bookmarks are not supported, but standard password access is provided, and multimedia links can be embedded in the courseware. E-mail and newsgroup class forums are asynchronous. A synchronous whiteboard facility is available through the use of NetTutor or

NetGroup from Link-Systems International. Learner self-assessment is accomplished through self-scoring quizzes, and scores are posted to the server. Learners can create their own Web portfolios and link them to Web projects.

Instructor Tools

Multiple instructors can edit or manage a class. Classes can be copied between instructor accounts, and instructors have the ability to track learner access to course pages. Web Course in a Box provides a feature called Faculty Home Page Builder to help instructors design instructional content.

Technical/Administrative Tools

Learner and instructor accounts can be batch uploaded, and there is a "Super User" account. Instructors can help perform troubleshooting by logging in as any user without restarting the program.

Technical Information

Web Course in a Box runs on Windows NT and Unix. The minimum client browser recommended is Netscape 2.0 or equivalent. Startup costs are free, and technical support is currently (1999) US$ 3,000 per year.

Course Info and Campus
(http://product.blackboard.net/courseinfo/)

CourseInfo was developed by Blackboard. The CMS can be installed locally at an institution or run from secure servers owned and operated by Blackboard. *Campus* is their new enterprise level product.

Learner Tools

CourseInfo is accessible from any Web browser. Learners can communicate asynchronously through e-mail and threaded discussions, or in real-time using Web chat forums and shared whiteboards. Learners can be organized into course Study Groups, with each group having its own bulletin board, chat forum, on-line file exchange, and e-mail distribution list. There is an on-line tutorial on how the product operates. Learners have access to a Course Calendar and Announcements, and entries can be made by learners and instructors, with course-specific entries, learner-specific entries, and shared entries.

Campus provides an on-line personal information manager called *My Blackboard* that provides a comprehensive view of calendar and course events, links to their on-line courses, and access to a virtual campus entity called University Center. The University Center provides access to all the administrative resources of *Campus*, such as Registrar and Bursar, and a learner union where faculty and learners can create interest groups and interact online.

Campus' Forum provides users with asynchronous and online communication and collaboration tools—threaded discussions that support file attachment, on-line chat, whiteboards, file transfer and storage areas, and group e-mail capabilities.

Instructor Tools

CourseInfo allows for the automatic sequencing of linked course documents, the reordering and searching of course content. Instructors have access to assessment tools and an electronic gradebook for providing feedback to students as well as automatic grading. Learners' progress is tracked by the system, and course statistics are provided. Instructors can also import pre-built course sites.

The use of *CourseInfo* requires no knowledge of HTML or other programming languages. Using simple point and click operations, instructors and course developers can incorporate learning materials from word processors, audio and video files, and presentation software. Blackboard provides a tool that allows for the streaming of audio and video files without the need for Internet plug-in software.

Campus' Course Manager is the core of the CMS, and is based on *CourseInfo's* course engine. Course Manager provides an easy-to-use control panel for creating and managing Web-based course sites without having to know HTML. The Course Builder facility provides instructors with tools for uploading content from any multimedia file format, and the ability to cut and paste information from existing documents or existing on-line courses, link Web pages, or insert audio and video without any programming skills.

Campus' Assessment facility provides an engine for the creation, delivery, and management of several types of on-line exams, including major tests, periodic "checks," self-assessment quizzes, and course surveys.

Technical/Administrative Tools

CourseInfo provides a System Administrator control panel, with the ability to copy, move, import, and export courses. There is a backup and restore capability, and courses can be managed online from any browser. The System Administrator can create and delete learner accounts, and there is a system logout feature for security purposes.

The *Campus* Content Server is a university-wide digital library of reusable content. Instructors will be able to index learning materials in this central location, and enable access to those materials from within multiple course sites.

Learner data and performance statistics are tracked with Campus' Profile Server. The information provided by Profile Server shows the learners' level of participation in discussions, assignments, and group activities, test performance, and allows the organization to track other course-related metrics.

Technical Information

For those organizations that do not have the technical infrastructure or expertise to host their own CMS, Blackboard provides pricing plans for course site hosting. Instructors and administrators still maintain total ownership and control over course content without the headache of maintaining the infrastructure it operates on. Course administrators access their courses through a private gateway page, and the top level Web site for the organization can be tailored visually for each organization. There is no limit to the number of courses, instructors, or learners that can be accommodated, and there are no per-user fees.

Campus is database and Web server platform independent, and will run on Windows NT and Unix, and is highly scalable. The Campus architecture is based on an enterprise database, a Web-based application layer, and access from a "thin client" Web browser.

Summary

These were summary descriptions of six popular COTS products. Most of the products are updated on a regular basis, and their Web sites (provided next to their name) provide the most accurate and up-to-date information about current features and functions, as well as announcements of future releases. Table 5.4 provides a summary of the features of each of the product.

Table 5.4 Summary of Feature/Tool Comparisons

Y=yes   F=future

Features/Tools	Learning Space	WebCT	Top Class	Tool book	Webcourse in a Box	Course Info
LEARNER TOOLS						
Web browsing						
• Accessibility						
• Bookmarks	Y	Y	Y	Y		Y
• Multimedia	Y	Y	Y		Y	Y
• Security	Y	Y	Y		Y	Y
Asynchronous sharing						
• E-mail	Y	Y	Y	Y	Y	Y
• BBS file exchange	Y	Y	Y			Y
• Newsgroups	Y	Y	Y	Y	Y	Y
Synchronous sharing						
• Chat	Y	Y		Y		Y
• Whiteboard	Y			Y	Y	F
• Application sharing	Y			Y		F
• Virtual space						F
• Group browsing	Y			Y		F
• Teleconferencing	Y			Y		F
• Videoconferencing	Y			Y		F
Student tools						
• Self-assessing	Y	Y	Y		Y	Y
• Progress tracking	Y	Y	Y	Y		Y
• Motivation building	Y	Y	Y		Y	Y
• Study skill building	Y	Y	Y			Y

Table 5.4 Summary of Feature/Tool Comparisons continued

Y=yes   F=future

Features/Tools	Learning Space	WebCT	Top Class	Tool book	Webcourse in a Box	Course Info
INSTRUCTOR TOOLS						
Course tools						
• Course planning	Y	Y	Y			Y
• Course managing	Y	Y	Y	Y	Y	Y
• Rapid course revising	Y	Y	Y	Y	Y	Y
• Course monitoring	Y	Y	Y	Y	Y	Y
Lesson tools						
• Instructional designing	Y	Y	Y	Y	Y	Y
• Presenting information	Y	Y	Y	Y		Y
• Testing	Y	Y	Y	Y		Y
Data tools						
• Marking online	Y	Y	Y			Y
• Managing records	Y	Y	Y			Y
• Analyzing and tracking	Y	Y	Y	Y	Y	Y
Resource tools						
• Building knowledge	Y	Y	Y			Y
• Team building	Y	Y	Y			Y
• Building motivation	Y		Y			
Reusable content tools			Y			

Table 5.4 Summary of Feature/Tool Comparisons continued

Y=yes   F=future

Features/Tools	Learning Space	WebCT	Top Class	Tool book	Webcourse in a Box	Course Info
TECHNICAL/ADMIN TOOLS						
Installation tools						
• Server	Y	Y	Y	Y		Y
• Client	Y			Y		
Help Desk tools						
• Student support tools	Y	Y	Y			Y
• Instructor support tools	Y	Y	Y		Y	Y
System tools						
• Authorization tools	Y	Y	Y		Y	Y
• Security tools	Y	Y	Y			Y
• Resource monitoring	Y	Y	Y			Y
• Remote access tools	Y	Y	Y			Y
• Crash recovery tools	Y	Y				Y
TECHNICAL INFO						
Server platform						
• RAM	Y	Y	Y	Y		Y
• Disk space	Y	Y		Y	Y	Y
• Windows NT 4.0	Y	Y	Y	Y	Y	F
• Apple server			Y			
• UNIX server	Y	Y	Y	Y	Y	Y
Client platform						
• Minimum level	Y	Y	Y	Y	Y	Y
• Target level	Y	Y	Y	Y	Y	Y
Pricing						
• Startup cost	Y	Y	Y		Y	Y
• Ongoing cost	Y	Y	Y			Y
• Technical support		Y			Y	Y
Limitations of package						
• Number of courses						Y
• Number of students		Y				Y
• Number of connections			Y			Y
• Number of instructors						Y
• Other limitations	Y	Y	Y	Y	Y	Y
Extra considerations						
• Options	Y					Y
• Exit considerations			Y			
• IMS project participant	Y	Y				Y

Chapter VI

Distance Learning Implementation and Evaluation

The implementation phase of a DL or technology insertion initiative begins after 1) the results of the feasibility analysis indicate whether, and to what extent, your courses should be converted to DL, or whether they could benefit from technology insertion into existing classrooms, 2) design considerations have been worked out, and 3) development has been done with existing staff resources or contractor support. This chapter outlines the issues, processes and practical tips for implementing and evaluating your DL initiative.

MANAGING YOUR DISTANCE LEARNING INITIATIVE

A critical success factor in implementing a DL initiative is to consciously manage the effort from its inception. This is not an understatement. Many DL initiatives begin as small efforts by motivated individuals outside of the strategic planning process, with little or no support or funding. These small successes usually result in a "bandwagon" phenomena, where significant financial resources are made available, and the DL imperative takes off with a life of its own, but without a well-thought-out strategic plan, or in some cases, without a feasibility study to see whether, in fact, all courses are actually suitable for DL. Sometimes early successes using one particular DL technology becomes an imperative to convert all courses to that particular technology, without consideration for whether or not that technology (with its capabilities and limitations) is actually the most appropriate for all courses. The result from these snowballing efforts based on isolated small successes can be some wasted effort, lack of strategy for reusable content, lack of priorities about which courses to convert first or how to coordinate the conversion effort with an infrastructure upgrade.

There are several strategic ways that a viable, effective DL initiative can be developed and managed. They include developing a strategic planning process for education and training, publishing a strategic education and training plan, tying in the strategic planning process to the budgeting and funding processes, developing metrics for tracking and analyzing investments made towards DL, taking time and effort to bring along all stakeholders in the DL initiative, and managing DL projects using standard project management techniques.

A Strategic Plan for Education and Training

When organizations tighten their budgets, training is often the very first thing to get knocked off because the purpose and value of training are not articulated in the organization's overall strategy. As we enter the 21st century, terms like "continual training," "lifelong learning," "knowledge workers," and "learning organization" are used to portray the importance of continual learning to successful performance on the job. In such an environment, training becomes an organizational imperative to maintaining competitive advantage—yet, it is likely the first budget category to be eliminated in a financial downturn. Eliminating training opportunities for organizational personnel is equivalent to throwing away an investment—we give up the possibility of a larger yield from the status quo.

Addressing education and training needs of the workforce in the organization's strategic plan can help orient senior decision makers to the importance of this investment. The training imperative should be tied to the organization's needs, priorities, competitive threats and opportunities. If a DL program is initiated, then the organization's strategic plan should clearly outline the expected benefits and returns on investment.

Budgeting for the DL Initiative

One–time conversion costs for DL are expensive. The payback or return on investment can be calculated in terms of cost avoidance, increased throughput, or a more capable workforce. A feasible way to manage the high cost of DL conversion is to phase out an investment plan over two to three years. It is difficult to estimate and plan for information technology beyond a three-year horizon because technology evolves so rapidly that we cannot always predict where advancements will be made, and the cost of technology in general is declining. It would be unwise to make a long-term commitment to any product or architecture, particularly if they do not adhere to open standards. A modular approach to implementing a standards-based, open architecture DL is a "safe bet" when committing to a long-term plan of investment.

Program Management of the DL Initiative

As important as the development of a strategic plan that is tied to a mid-term investment plan, it is also critical to take a program management approach to any DL conversion initiative. At a minimum, the following steps should be taken to establish your DL program management.

Identify all Stakeholders

It is common for the group of people who first become acquainted with the potential for DL to be different than the group of people who are the senior decision makers, and they are different than the group of people influential in controlling the funding for strategic initiatives. There are usually others groups of important stakeholders, including the instructors in the traditional classroom environment and finally, but most importantly, the learners.

Understand the Interests, Role and Responsibilities of Each Stakeholder Group

Each stakeholder group has an important role and function in the overall success of your DL initiative. Each group has something different to gain or to lose (in their perception) from the initiative.

Develop an Earned Value Approach to Managing Your DL Projects

Many organizations use combined in-house and contractor support as they progress through analysis, design, development, implementation and evaluation phases. Setting up an earned value management system (EVMS) to track progress and resources expended helps program and project managers to keep senior decision makers informed about real progress on conversion projects.

Use Change Management and Organizational Communication Processes to Get and Maintain Stakeholder Support

Given the diversity of perspectives inherent in a multiple stakeholder environment, it is important to develop a communication process for keeping all stakeholders informed of the benefits of DL, the progress made on the initiative and to resolve any issues or concerns.

Change Management and Organizational Communication Requirements

Resistance to the concept of DL includes concerns by learners that they will not have contact or feedback from instructors; fears by instructors that their role (and jobs) are in jeopardy; skepticism about the effectiveness of DL technologies and learning retention; dislike of using computer technologies; and, perception that learning objectives or instructional integrity of the course will be compromised if it is converted to a DL format.

It is vital that the organization have an organized method by which it disseminates accurate and concise information about the similarities and differences of a DL environment from the traditional classroom. It should also clearly discuss how current learning objectives (i.e., getting feedback from the instructor, or interacting with other learners) can be accomplished through the use of asynchronous and synchronous DL technologies.

One of the most effective ways to tackle the change management effort in the transition to a DL environment is to use a prototype or pilot approach to conversion. In prototype development, users work with developers and course designers to iteratively develop and implement a DL course. User/learner feedback is critical to the final design of the product, and helps smooth the way for implementation.

Project Management Considerations

A distance learning initiative requires the orchestration of personnel with diverse skill sets—people who, in a traditional classroom environment, have almost nothing to do with one another. For example, a DL project requires subject matter experts (SMEs) and instructional systems designers to work with highly technical graphics artists, videographers, Web programmers, network specialists and multimedia production specialists. Managing a project with a diverse project team requires a project manager who has:

- Technical knowledge ranging from Web development, multimedia tools, data communications, instructional design, reusable content warehousing and course management systems.
- Business skills to manage the financial resources and the staffing mix.
- Project management skills to identify, decompose, and integrate all sub-tasks in the work breakdown structure.
- Interpersonal skills to keep this diverse group working as a team and the ability to resolve technical, financial, and interpersonal conflicts.
- Strategic focus to keep the project moving towards the larger organizational requirements.

Many large initiatives end up on shaky ground when project managers are not qualified or experienced in all of the above areas—they may have been assigned the project because of technical skills alone or because of responsibilities in the financial area. It is a worthwhile investment for a large initiative to have a senior, experienced project manager, particularly if the conversion involves groups of courses or an entire curriculum.

Implementing the Virtual Campus:
Administrative Requirements

Conversion of an entire curriculum of courses requires a method or process to manage the administrative overhead associated with course management. The administrative processes that occur in a traditional campus environment are also required to support faculty, staff, and students in a virtual campus environment.

Registrar functions

The function of the registrar's office is to plan, schedule, and coordinate all courses offered in the curriculum. A major aspect of traditional registration that may not be as critical in the virtual environment is the complex course scheduling process that occurs. Courses, student requirements, time slots, and instructor availability must all be considered in the makeup of the time schedules. With the exception of synchronous activities, time slots are not as critical in the virtual university. However, the registrar's responsibility for planning and developing the list of course offerings remains, as well as the assignments of instructors to courses.

Bursar functions

The term Bursar is used here as an umbrella term to include student financial services, billing, financial aid, payroll services, and contracts. In a virtual university environment, students will enroll in courses, make payments and other transactions using a Web-based interface.

Student Center

Learners gather in the student center to read and distribute announcements, to visit/meet with other learners for social and learning activities, attend campus-sponsored events, etc. The virtual equivalent of the Student Center would provide bulletin boards for listing information, listservers for disseminating information, Web chat forums for group interaction, and streaming audio/video for "attending" scheduled speeches or other events.

Campus Information / Admissions

Most campuses now have Web sites that are their "front door" to their campuses. A virtual campus is the same; in fact from a campus' "front door" Web site, it is not always obvious at first glance whether the organization is virtual or a traditional brick and mortar campus.

Technology Support / Academic Computing

Academic computing services provides the technology support

infrastructure to everyone within the campus—students, faculty, staff, and other administrative personnel. In a virtual campus, the role of academic computing would be a support function for the on-line environment—managing the applications, servers, communication technologies, as well as providing technical support to the users of the system, whether they are instructors or students.

Faculty Support

On traditional campuses, the administration provides faculty with support in several ways. They provide instructional systems designers to work with instructors to design their curriculum; faculty are provided with tools, supplies and classroom equipment (e.g., projectors, whiteboards) to support instructional activities in the classroom. Faculty support also includes financial resources to attend conferences, present papers and conduct research. The virtual campus must support its faculty in some new ways. Faculty must be provided with new tools and technologies for conducting their on-line courses, but they will still require traditional types of support mentioned above.

These requirements do not go away in a DL environment. The most effective way to establish these functions for DL courses is to incorporate them into the DL environment. Many COTS packages offer Web-based functionality similar to these traditional educational functions. Learners are able to view course catalogs, register, enroll, and participate in on-line learning environments while having access to these traditional "functions" and roles in learning institutions.

EMERGING TREND: HYBRID DELIVERY METHODS

After completing a feasibility analysis, most courses that are eligible for DL conversion are also eligible for more than one type of delivery. Each type of delivery has associated benefits, costs, and limitations, as discussed in chapters three and four. There are compelling reasons why many organizations are moving toward a hybrid strategy using both WBT and CBT as delivery mechanisms for courseware. WBT and CBT complement each other's strengths and minimize each other's weaknesses. Used in combination, hybrid delivery offers many advantages for the learner, instructor, course designer, course developer, program managers, and financial planners. It is increasingly cost effective and easy to plan, budget and implement for hybrid delivery.

Advantages of a Hybrid Delivery Strategy
to the Learner and Instructor

A hybrid delivery strategy is learner-centric and meets the needs of students anywhere in the world, whether at work, in the field, at a learning center, or at home.

Increased Access to Training

A hybrid delivery strategy provides assurance that instruction can be delivered to learners anytime, anywhere. If learners have access to the Internet from a workstation with the appropriate plug-ins, they can download and access courseware from a local learning center server or from other remote servers around the world.

Improves Learner Productivity

In the workplace, learner productivity is a function of the learner's availability to accomplish job-related tasks and the ability to demonstrate required knowledge and skills to perform the job. If a learner spends too much time away for training, then on-the-job productivity is reduced for that period of time. This can cause minor or major disruptions in planning and operations in the work environment. In an era of organizational "right-sizing", there are few personnel with duplicate skills in any work group. The loss of a team member's presence can negatively impact the productivity of other personnel in the office who work on collaborative tasks where individuals contribute a particular area of expertise. On the other hand, if the learner is never allowed time off for training, the knowledge and skill levels required to perform current or future jobs will be lacking, and the professional advancement of personnel will be diminished.

DL helps increase learner productivity by improving both processes. First, the learner is away from the work assignment for a shorter period of time (due to compression factors) and may even be able to arrange a part-time work/study situation while taking a DL course at his or her desktop or in the organization's learning center. Second, the learner can enroll in DL courses as part of a "lifelong learning" program and be continually refreshed in knowledge of the career field.

Improves Instructor Productivity

The Defense Acquisition University (DAU) is an example of using a hybrid WBT/CBT delivery strategy to increase instructor productivity. Each of their on-line courses (also available on CD-ROM by mail) has several thousand students enrolled at any given time, and more than several hundred students per instructor. The resulting student/instructor ratio is much higher than could be accommodated in a physical classroom, given the type and level of interaction and feedback between students and instructors. Instructors conduct office hours on-line (synchronously and asynchronously) and are able to monitor and help students with their performance through the on-line testing facility and course managed instruction (CMI) system. This level of support and interaction would limit a traditional classroom-based instructor to no more than 50 students. By contrast, the enrollment of potentially thousands of students in a course means that instructors are significantly more productive in providing services to students than teachers in the traditional classroom environment.

Ensures Instructional Consistency

When different instructors teach a course, or when instructors teach multiple sections, particularly in education where course modules are not as structured, it is common that the course material is delivered inconsistently. In institutions of higher education, the choice of one's professor (given the same syllabus, textbook, and exams) often makes a great deal of difference in terms of student learning, motivation, appreciation of the topic and ability to apply the material in work or other academic areas. A hybrid WBT/CBT delivery strategy provides consistency in presentation and delivery of the instructional content. The extensive instructional design process during the creation of WBT/CBT ensures that course objectives, instructional goals, and the instructional content are presented in the most effective formats.

Increases Motivation to Learn

The use of WBT/CBT delivery supported by computer-mediated communication (CMC) technologies provides learners and instructors with a very rich communication and learning environment.

Increased learner engagement with instructional content is correlated with increased motivation to learn (McArdle, 1999; Mantyla and Guiden, 1997).

Increases Mastery of Material

When instructional content is presented in multiple formats, learners are able to absorb the material using more than one sensory mode. Research indicates that using multiple senses to make mental associations helps in the recall of that material (Hall, 1997; Ivers and Barron, 1998).

Course-Managed Instruction

One limitation of CBT delivery that is mitigated with WBT is the use of CMI to track learner performance. With the exception of learners who do not have access to the Internet and must complete courseware entirely offline, the use of a dual delivery strategy makes the development and use of CMI possible. CMI is software that supports administration and management of the course. CMI can provide information concerning learner performance trends (per learner, for the class, or across class sections), capture and record individual and group performance information. The instructor is able to use CMI to identify and diagnose performance deficiencies and also to improve the effectiveness of test design.

Advantages of a Hybrid Delivery Strategy to Course Designers and Developers

Most vendors of CBT courseware tools understand the power and potential of WBT and have modified their tools such that courseware designed in their tool can be published for WBT delivery. Additionally, recent improvements in CD-ROM technologies make possible the "burning" or reproduction of CD-ROMs easily and cost effectively. Courseware can be developed for dual delivery to suit learners' requirements. Tools such as CMS described above provide a seamless and integrated collaborative environment for course designers, course developers, instructors and administrators.

Advantages of a Hybrid Delivery Strategy to Program Managers and Financial Planners

Implementing a hybrid delivery strategy is relatively simple because of the similarities in cost factors used for estimating, planning, and budgeting purposes:

Compression factors. Studies show that both WBT and CBT achieve similar compression rates (between 25 and 35 percent). The compression rate is calculated as a percentage of traditional classroom instruction hours that can be deducted from the length of a course delivered by traditional delivery methods.

Development hours to convert. Studies show that the number of hours to develop each hour of courseware is approximately the same for WBT and CBT (Level I courseware=50 hours, Level II courseware=265, Level III courseware=700).

Skill sets required. The types and levels of technical skills required for WBT and CBT design and development are similar, given that emerging development tools have the capability for dual delivery.

Instructional systems design process. The ISD process is almost identical for WBT and CBT delivery. Storyboards, sequencing, and branching scenarios must be developed, and multimedia files (audio, video, graphics) can be developed for either type of delivery.

Ease of update. Updating of courseware is much easier to accomplish with WBT delivery because new content can be sent out to user and learning center servers. For those learners without Internet access, updated courseware or materials can be sent to the local learning center, where an updated CD-ROM can be produced and delivered to them. Course Web sites can provide information on the latest updates or versions to staff and learners.

Technology Insertion

Some course objectives require the instructor's physical presence with the learners. These courses may benefit from technology insertion. The question is, "when is technology insertion appropriate, and does it pay off from an economic standpoint?" Technology insertion into the traditional classroom environment can have a tremendous impact on training quality, learning retention and cost avoidance. On-line course materials can:

- Reinforce teacher-provided instruction.
- Provide synchronous communication opportunities outside of the classroom for learners and the instructor to interact.
- Provide opportunity for self-paced remediation.

- Provide opportunity for online self-testing and self-help.
- Provide the instructor with the ability to monitor and track learners' progress in an unobtrusive way.
- Provide the instructor with the opportunity to provide feedback, encouragement and rewards to learners using multiple communication means.

TRANSITIONING TO A DISTANCE LEARNING ENVIRONMENT

Whether the instructor is inserting technology into the learning environment, or whether a transition is being made to a DL environment, there are some tasks to accomplish before and during this time.

Train the Trainer

For combined delivery (traditional classroom and DL) or for technology insertion, the instructors require training in the application and use of WBT and CBT delivery and in the use of instructor tools. Unless the instructors have extensive information technology experience, particularly in Web-based and multimedia technologies, they will require training in the use of course authoring tools, course management utilities and general technical support. The most effective way to bring instructors "online" is to include them as active participants early in the conversion project. They provide important feedback about instructional goals and activities, while having the opportunity to become acquainted with the application of advanced instructional technologies to the classroom.

Preparing the Learning Center

Learning Centers (also called multimedia resource centers, learning labs, computer center for students) are facilities designed to house many learner workstations. They are usually equipped with multimedia PCs, high resolution monitors, speakers and CD-ROM drives. They may also be equipped with desktop cameras and microphones for desktop audio or video conferencing. Each Learning Center is supported by one or more personnel on a technical staff, whose responsibilities include:

- Installing and maintaining all hardware, peripherals and software configurations of the workstations in the Learning Center

(LC).

- Troubleshooting problems for all workstations in the LC.
- Managing and monitoring the schedule for use of the LC.
- Maintaining the library of CD-ROMs and other courseware for use by learners in the LC.
- Maintaining and providing usage statistics for the facility for planners and other decision makers.
- Providing assistance and training on the use of the workstations for CBT or WBT delivery.
- If the facility also supports courseware maintenance, then they provide instructors or course designers with technical support and (optional) use of shared resources, such as scanners, CD-ROM burners, audio/video recording equipment.

Organizing Support Materials

As courseware is developed, there will be a large accumulation of images, icons, digitized photos, graphics, audio clips, video clips, as well as hard copies of CDs, films, photos and other images that have been digitized. Two types of repositories should be organized. One is the physical repository of courseware materials that can be indexed and reused by other courseware developers. The other is the electronic repository of multimedia files that serve as the bank of reusable "raw" courseware materials. This electronic repository of multimedia files is different than the repository of completed instructional modules/objects, which serves as the learning content repository.

UPGRADING YOUR INFRASTRUCTURE TO SUPPORT DISTANCE LEARNING

A DL environment can include the home, school, workplace, learning lab, library or other facility. For each type of learning situation, there are minimum requirements for hardware, software, connectivity and other resources.

Instruction delivered at the desktop (without any internal or external connectivity to other devices) is referred to as Computer-Based Training (CBT). It requires a multimedia capable personal computer with a CD-ROM or DVD drive. The typical user interface for desktop delivered instruction is a multimedia application or a Web browser reading HTML files from a CD-ROM.

Assessing Your Current Infrastructure

The questionnaire in Appendix C will help you ascertain an overall picture of your existing infrastructure, and what areas need upgrading. There are seven sections in this inventory.

Internet Requirements

For WBT, access to the Internet is required. In addition to finding out if all learners have access to the Internet, it is important to know what type of access they have, the speed of the connection, and whether or not they have an Internet e-mail account. If they share this Internet connectivity, it is important to find out if the aggregate bandwidth is sufficient to support additional learners for on-line courses.

Desktop/LAN Requirements

There are several important issues for desktop/LAN requirements, which revolve around having sufficient capability to run CBT or synchronous WBT applications. First, the processor of the desktop computer must be fast enough, and there must be sufficient storage for large multimedia files. Second, users will likely require the ability to use plug-ins at their desktop PC, so if the organization prohibits the downloading, installation, or use of plug-ins, the type of courseware will be limited to level 1 (text and graphics only). Third, the user's PC must be equipped with multimedia accessories to be able to play audio/video clips and must be equipped with camera and microphone to participate in collaboration software. Fourth, LAN connectivity provides the potential to use collaborative software, and access to a server is required. The shared file server provides the ability to store and access files collaboratively without having to send them through e-mail as attachments.

Collaboration Requirements

Special software applications are required to run a collaborative environment. A dedicated server must be available to host the software and associated files so that learners can participate in real-time collaborative tasks.

User Support Requirements

Users require Help Desk support, and the response time for trouble calls must be within the tolerance level of the learners, or they will lose interest and motivation to fully use the instructional technologies. If a learning environment is operated globally, or if learners access the courseware at any time, then Help Desk hours will need to be extended to cover the users during those times.

Video/Interactive TV Requirements

Broadcasting and receiving video and interactive TV requires facilities at the broadcast site (uplink) and a classroom with enough seats for all learners at the receiving (downlink) site. Satellite time is very expensive, and the existing schedule for leased time must be checked before planning additional courses. If classes are recorded for rebroadcast at remote sites, then a video library must be set up.

Video Teleconferencing

As discussed in chapter three, video teleconferencing is very expensive and generally suitable only for small classes or group meetings. The cost, features, and functions of the TC system can vary. The critical factor is the studio/classroom capacity for the TC system (mikes, camera coverage) and the number of hours available for TC use.

Computer Learning Center/Lab

A computer learning center or lab is a facility where learners can go to use multimedia PCs and work through CBT or use the Internet for WBT. The learning center/lab must be equipped with hardware and software that can access and run all types of CBT. The learner to computer ratio of an organization should be low enough so that learners can participate in instruction at their convenience.

EVALUATING DISTANCE LEARNING

Chapter one introduced some important questions managers, educators and administrators must ask before, during and after implementation of DL. Some of the questions are reproduced here.

- What do we get out of our investments in DL?
- Will our employees be better trained in DL? Or at least, will they

be as well trained as in our traditional learning environments?
- What can we do to increase the likelihood that our DL programs will be successful?
- How do we evaluate the success of our DL programs?

As was discussed briefly during the presentation of the "ADDIE" model in chapter four, evaluation is a task that occurs throughout the lifecycle of the project. There are many benefits to doing evaluation as a continuous process.

Benefits of Evaluation

Doing life cycle evaluation has three main benefits. First, it is the only way to determine whether or not, and to what degree, instructional objectives have been met. Second, it is the only way to determine, post hoc, what the actual return on investment has been. Third, evaluation results provide valuable feedback so that the program can be continually improved.

Summative vs. Formative Evaluation

There are two basic types of evaluation, summative and formative.

Summative Evaluation

Summative evaluation is a final assessment of a product, service, or process. A summative evaluation summarizes the results of a completed study. Since evaluation is done on a continuing basis throughout the lifecycle, the appropriate type of evaluation for DL projects is formative evaluation.

Formative Evaluation

The primary purpose of formative evaluation is to improve the product, service, or process as it is being developed. Formative evaluation has a long and rich tradition in the assessment of instructional technologies, beginning with formative evaluation studies for development of "Sesame Street" to studies of adoption of new communication technologies (Williams, Rice and Rogers, 1988).

There are several useful models of formative evaluation that can be used to perform continual evaluation of the instructional design and conversion lifecycle (described in the following sub-sections).

Each of these models provide insight on variables to consider in one or more steps of the evaluation process (Williams, Rice and Rogers, 1988).

Define the objectives of the evaluation. For example, one can use Marshall and Shriver's (1994) five-level evaluation model that allows for evaluation of the instructor, course materials, curriculum, course module, and learning transfer.

Select the scope of the research. The Van Slyke, Kittner and Belanger framework (1998) can be used to conceptualize the "as is" environment that the learner is embedded in—the institution, the learner, the course, and the type(s) of DL technologies applied. Evaluation studies do not have to capture and analyze all these variables, but the evaluator should understand that these are factors that interact to impact learners in DL. An evaluation program should explicitly define which of these categories of variables are being measured, which are being controlled for, and what the outcome variables are.

Select the data gathering method(s). There are many different types of formative data-gathering methods, some of which will be briefly outlined in this chapter. They include individual questionnaires, personal interviews, focus groups, and observation. For example, Kirkpatrick's (1994) four-level evaluation model can be used to focus on different aspects of learning outcomes ranging from affective "reaction" to organizational "results."

Models of Formative Evaluation

Van Slyke et al. (1998) Framework

A framework for distance education proposed by Van Slyke, Kittner and Belanger (1998) suggests that multiple variables must be taken into account concurrently in looking at their effect on DL. Their framework looks at determinants of success (precedent variables) and evaluation criteria (outcome variables). Determinants of success can be grouped into four categories of variables:

Institutional Characteristics. The variables in this category relate to the organization. Some examples include objectives, delivery mechanisms, and support structure. The objectives of the institution for establishing a DL program, such as to cut cost or to increase reach, will affect the likelihood of success of the program. The delivery mechanisms are another institutional characteristic that will have an impact.

These include the technology infrastructures available for delivering the material. For example, some organizations made an early commitment to delivery via VTT. With recent technological advances in Web-based delivery, WBT delivery may provide features and benefits of DL that were not possible with VTT. More importantly, learners who are familiar with the synchronous communication capabilities of the Web may not be satisfied to receive training passively in VTT mode. Finally, the support structure will also have an important role to play (for example, will learners have a 24-hour a day help line if they have problems with their cybercourses?).

Learner Characteristics. Some of the variables relating to the learner include objectives and skills. Objectives of the learner play an important role in determining likelihood of success in a distance or distributed learning environment for particular learners. For example, if learners want to participate in DL because of expectations that doing so requires less work than traditional learning, the likelihood of their success may decrease. Similarly, it is expected that personal skills of the learners such as self-sufficiency, computer proficiency, time management, interpersonal communication, problem solving, and planning, will affect DL outcomes. Previous technology experience and expectations also affect learners' preconceived attitudes towards DL.

Course Characteristics. Several important characteristics of the course itself should be taken into consideration before attempting to convert material from a lecture based environment to a DL environment. A common course requirement in the information systems curriculum in universities is the group project, for example, for software development courses. Group projects require collaboration and interdependence among the learners; therefore, careful planning prior to conversion to a DL environment must be accomplished in order to preserve the key characteristics of the learning environment. For example, for courses that require group projects, a suite of computer-mediated communication (CMC) technologies could be used to support collaboration tasks. Other course characteristics that should be examined include evaluation methods, and hands-on components in the course. The characteristics of the course, the learner and the technology must "fit" for effective learning to occur (see Figure 6.1).

Distance Learning Characteristics. One of the most important characteristics of today's DL context is the extensive use of technology. As such, the level and type of technology available for DL is an important

Figure 6.1 Framework for Distance Education and Training

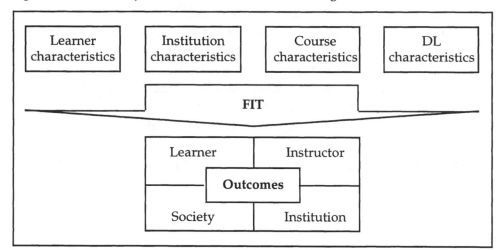

characteristic in determining the likelihood of success in implementing such programs. Another variable within the DL category is the environment of the learner. Learners attending classes in traditional classroom environments have a set time with a set place that is relatively quiet and conducive to learning—the kind of environment that has been termed "right time, right place" environments. Making a transition to a "anytime, anywhere" environment provides no inherent guarantees for quiet, comfort, and ease of learning. These are factors that become the responsibility of the learner and the providing organization. New models of work/study may need to be developed to accommodate workers who pursue learning in a DL environment.

All of these characteristics and variables must be carefully examined, not in isolation, but together in evaluating the appropriateness for an individual, a course, and an organization to attend, convert, or implement DL. Van Slyke et al. also suggest that there are two levels of outcomes and two measures of success: one for institutions and one for students. We want to extend the model to include four different units of analysis impacted by DL: the learner, the instructor, the institution, and society. The adapted framework is presented in Figure 6.1.

The figure shows that the outcomes of DL can be found at multiple levels. Examples of outcomes for the learner include increased technology awareness and skills, higher quality of interaction with the teacher, or better access to instructor. Note that the outcomes for one learner can be different than for another learner, depending on how the characteristics on the top of the model interact. Institutional outcomes include lower costs of providing education, increased reach to potential learners, increased productivity among instructors and the sharing of instructional resources with other institutions. Finally, there may be outcomes at the societal level such as a more professional workforce, increased quality of life and increased access to education (regardless of culture, social class or financial status of the family).

Marshall and Shriver's Five Levels of Evaluation [from McArdle, 1999, p. 138]

Marshall and Shriver's (1994) five-level model is performance-based and requires the learner to demonstrate knowledge and skills.

Self. Even in a DL environment, where instructors may be separated from their students by time and/or distance, it is necessary to get feedback from learners about the instructor's performance. The DL environment presents both opportunities and challenges for instructors because their "persona" may be projected only through the medium of course Web pages, Web chat forums and e-mail. In these cases, it is important that the instructor understand the constraints of using communication media to communicate with learners. Projecting a responsive, supportive persona in the DL environment may be a challenge for instructors who cannot effectively project their desired persona through these technologies (e.g., projecting concern, warmth, competence is as important for virtual instructors as it is in the traditional classroom).

Course materials. Learners' comments about the course materials is valuable for improving the course—the level of difficulty, interest, or overall effectiveness of the course content.

Course curriculum. Evaluating the course curriculum requires a higher order analysis, where multiple courses are evaluated and compared across the curriculum.

Course modules. Many instructors assign chapters in a textbook out of sequence because the topics fit better with their overall syllabus if they are rearranged. Likewise, the course modules can be assessed for the effectiveness of their structure and order.

Learning transfer. This level is a summary concept based on Kirkpatrick's (1994) four levels of learning transfer described below.

Kirkpatrick's Four Levels of Evaluation

Kirkpatrick's (1994) four levels of evaluation model is often used to evaluate the impact of the learning experience at affective, cognitive, behavioral and organizational levels. Definitions and examples are provided for each.

Level 1: Learner reaction. The evaluation at this level is affective in nature. Surveys, questionnaires, focus groups and interviews can be conducted to assess learners' reactions to instruction. The surveys can include questions that ask learners for their perception of the other levels, i.e., whether they achieved learning objectives, what impact they feel training might have on their performance, and so forth. The key point is that this is a personal reaction to the learning experience, and may or may not correspond with other more external measures of the impact of the learning experience.

Level 2: Knowledge transfer. Evaluations at this level measure what the participants have actually learned, both cognitively and in skills acquired. These evaluations are more difficult and time consuming to develop than learner reaction surveys, but they are essential for gauging the effectiveness of the learning experience against the learning objectives. Tests of knowledge transfer to the learner make up the traditional "testing" processes used in traditional and on-line courses. The types of knowledge transfer tests can range from recognition (multiple choice), recall (fill in the blanks; short answers), problem solving, essay questions, case study problems and practical application (e.g., create a spreadsheet). Tests of knowledge transfer should be done often in a DL course so that the learner can assess his/her progress and receive feedback and/or remediation.

Level 3: Behavior transfer. Assessment at this level are of observed and measurable behavioral changes in the learner. The practical impact of learning is often not measured in the traditional learning environment. At most, certification tests are given at the end of a curriculum or program of study, but one doesn't find out how effective the learner is unless he/she is evaluated on the job or other situation where the practical application of learning can be tested. Some practitioners suggest (Moore and Alvarez, 1999) that a control group or a pre-test and post-test of the target group should be used. Methods used to assess at this level can include 360 degree surveys (peers, subordinates, supervisors of the target employee), but sufficient time must be allowed for behavioral change to take place after training.

Level 4: Organizational impact. The unit of assessment changes at this level from individual to the organization. Organizational measures are used to capture return on investment or improved service response time, service quality, reduction in manufacturing defects, reduction in customer complaints, increased sales, and so forth. These are not explicit measures of causality but correlation between the impact of training and corresponding increase or reduction in organizational variables.

CONCLUDING COMMENTS

We have covered a lot of the DL landscape in this book. It is a continually evolving landscape with new tools, technologies, and applications each year. In spite of the rapid pace of advancements in technology, there are fundamental drivers in organizations, in the economy and in society that will continue to mandate the move towards more DL methods of instructional delivery. We hope that this book provided a solid introduction to the concepts, technologies and processes involved in considering a practical move towards DL conversion, or technology insertion into the classroom.

The drivers for enterprise-wide distance learning solutions for your organization that deliver opportunity, flexibility and responsive training include:

- *Need to lower training costs per learner.* There will be continuing pressure in both private and public sector organizations to reduce the costs of training while improving worker performance on the job. Many organizations have reduced budgets overall, and it is a well-known phenomena in the private industry and the government that when budgets are cut, training is its first victim.
- *Need to consider technology insertion into the traditional classroom.* Many DL technologies are suitable for insertion into traditional classroom environments where learning objectives require the presence of the instructor or face-to-face interaction. Combined use of traditional and DL technologies in the learning environment can reduce training infrastructure requirements, increase learner throughput through courses and enhance the retention of instructional content.

- *Need to integrate distance learning into existing training plans and strategies, outlining cost savings and/or cost avoidance that might be achieved through increased use of DL.* Organizations need to articulate how DL will impact existing training infrastructures in terms of requirements for instructors, equipment, etc. They will need to develop new cost estimating models to use in the distributed learning environment, where learners do not occupy the "seat" used in traditional cost estimation models.

Chapter VII

Examples of Distance Learning Evaluation and Implementation

OVERVIEW

This chapter presents three fictitious case studies of organizations facing decisions to convert one or several courses to distance learning. As you read through the cases, you will be presented with the issues that many real organizations face when trying to decide whether, and to what extent distance learning should be implemented in their organization. Two of the cases presented depict commercial organizations, and the third represents an higher education institution.

Each case presents background information on the organization, major stakeholders, and the current state of distance learning initiatives within the organization. Each case focuses on a different aspect of the analysis for distance learning. The first case covers the strategic analysis, the second presents a course conversion analysis, and the third presents an infrastructure analysis. Together, these should walk the reader through several analysis issues faced in real world situations.

CASE STUDY I: STRATEGIC ANALYSIS

Optima University
Background

Optima is a large urban private university with graduate and undergraduate colleges in arts & sciences, business, law, medicine, nursing, engineering, and communications. It is well-funded and well-positioned as one of the top institutions in the country. Its history of growth is similar to that of other public and private universities in the U.S. after World War II. The history of growth in U.S. institutions of higher learning is in part responsible for their current challenges to find new ways to serve their stakeholders while increasing their non-government funded revenues. Distance learning technologies represent one of the solutions to this challenge of broadening the base of learners.

The GI bill enabled millions of Americans who could not otherwise have afforded a college education to obtain one. Universities were then able to use the revenues from increased enrollments to fund capital investments in buildings, and to increase their faculty and staff. That, in turn, fueled the graduate and professional school enrollments. Returning servicemen and women from WWII also accomplished something else-they returned to normalcy after more than a decade that had seen the last few years of the Great Depression followed by the hardships of a world war. They began families in unprecedented numbers, causing the "Baby Boom" generation of individuals born between 1946 and the middle of the next decade.

The Baby Boomers entered college in the mid-60's, at a time when institutions of higher education were flush with revenue from the post-war growth and expansion. By the mid-70's this growth began to slow down. First, the population bulge of Baby Boomers were beyond the traditional "college age" of 18 to 22 years old. Second, American families had grown steadily smaller, leaving a smaller pool from which to draw the traditional student. By the late 90's applications and enrollments to the nation's top universities started rising again. This time, it is attributed to the sustained economic "boom" of the 90's, and the desire of Americans to get the best education possible for their children. However, despite this mini-boom, the reality is that the rising costs of higher education (over $30,000 per year for top schools) have far outpaced the increasing interest in these top schools.

Current Programs at Optima University

In response to the changing demographics in this country, institutions of higher learning like Optima University had to be entrepreneurial and highly responsive to the needs of their stake-holder community-students, faculty, staff, and alumni-in order to maintain revenue levels from college enrollment. They began to redefine the previous concept of the "college student" as an unmarried person between the ages of 18 and 22 who resided at a college and completed their degree in four years, and who left college never to return except for a graduate degree or to proudly usher in their children as the promising next generation. The new concept of "college student" included non-degree seeking learners, part-time learners, and "life-long" learners who participate in the learning process at each stage of their life. Optima and other universities began to offer revenue-generating programs to a much larger segment of the population, and the concept of "lifelong learning" began to take hold in this country. In addition to the traditional 4-year undergraduate and 2-year masters programs, Optima started offering the following set of "new" programs:

1. *Continuing Education Programs.* Continuing education programs offer non-credit courses for graduates and non-graduates who want to take courses but who are not enrolled in degree-granting programs. These accommodate working professionals, retirees, non-working mothers, and students who are interested in furthering their knowledge but who are not willing or able to pursue a particular degree in that area. Popular continuing-education programs at Optima include basic computer applications training, foreign language courses, and a large number of visual arts and "professional skills" courses (e.g., managerial accounting). Their list of continuing education courses, however, is not limited to these areas, and includes a variety of courses in horticulture, health sciences, and even music production.

2. *Evening Courses.* Evening courses are similar to continuing education courses in the way they are set up, except for the fact that the courses are the same as those offered in daytime slots, and are usually taken as part of a degree-granting program. These courses were established to accommodate students who work part-time or full-time, or who are engaged in sports activities during part of the day.

3. *Executive MBA Programs.* Executive MBA programs offer full-time senior managers and executives the opportunity to follow a professional program that leads to the MBA degree. These programs accommodate these senior managers and executives by offering classes that meet once a week on alternating Fridays and/or Saturdays.

4. *Coop Programs.* Coop programs are usually five-year degree-granting undergraduate programs in which one year is spent working as an intern at a public or private organization whose mission is focused in the student's field of study. Close ties between the institution and the participating organization are formed. There is mutual benefit from the student's ability to directly apply his/her knowledge base to actual work activities, and the organization's ability to obtain the benefits of inexpensive labor and a potential new hire upon graduation.

Distance Learning at Optima University

The current president of Optima University, Myriam Artema, has occupied her position for the last eight years She has been instrumental in seeing the University through the end of a high-growth period and the beginning of a period in which applications and enrollments began to level off, mirroring trends in other top universities in the country. She is currently particularly challenged with trying to maintain a balance between the high-growth areas, such as business and information technology programs, and the areas suffering from reductions in enrollments, such as history and art. Seeking opportunities to improve Optima's competitive position in the higher education market, she is starting to think that distance learning might be a solution to expand the reach to new students at Optima, and a way to enhance the quality of the educational experience at the school.

President Artema has challenged her Board of Regents to consider the possibilities and potential of distance learning programs at Optima, in the same way that the Board had considered whether and how to implement its other programs over the years (Coop, Executive MBA, combined degree programs, and continuing education).

The Board is now discussing the challenges and opportunities of distance learning at Optima. On the one hand, the high quality of resident-based education and the prestige of Optima's resident educational programs would be difficult to envision being delivered without the Ivy-covered buildings and famous walkways through campus. Optima has taken pride over the years that courses are taught by Professors and not graduate students, and Professors make themselves readily available to all students outside of class through office hours, appointments, email, and course Web sites.   It would be a challenge to provide that same level of time and quality, and "presence" of the university through a virtual medium. Is it possible, and how would that be accomplished?

On the other hand, many of Optima's graduates are not able to take advantage of the non-traditional programs being offered by the school. They are enrolled at other state, local, or private institutions in the evening, Executive MBA, and continuing education programs that are in cities closer to where they work and live. Would it be possible to offer them Optima's quality programs through distance learning? Doing so would allow Optima to provide educational services to a wider audience without requiring them to invest in more "brick and mortar" facilities on the campus.

Given that the Board and the President agree that the core business of Optima will continue to be offering high-quality educational programs to resident students in the classroom, they have ruled out total conversion of courses to a distance learning format. The Board is therefore considering partial conversion and technology insertion into the classroom as alternatives for distance learning implementation.

One surprise this year is that Optima experienced a higher than normal "yield" in its entering freshman class, as did most of the other top schools around the country. Admissions officers attribute this to the booming national economy-parents are able to send their children to the school of choice, as opposed to settling for the one that is the cheapest. As a result of this unexpected yield, administrators find that they have too few freshman seminars to accommodate the demand. Freshman seminars are a notable experience for incoming freshman at Optima, and over 80% elect to take either a writing or other topical seminar set up specifically for freshman. They are very small groups of 8-10 students, some choosing to meet in the residential dorms, and the topics generate lively exchange, foster deeper thinking into topics, and serve to "jump start" the freshmen into the rigors of college-level scholarship expected of them. How can Optima provide enough freshman seminars to accommodate the increased number of students, given the limitation in classroom space and student-to-teacher ratios necessary for the optimal "freshman experience"?

Evaluating Distance Learning at Optima

To address the question of whether, and to what extent, distance learning should be implemented at Optima University, President Artema and the Board of Regents held a special session where several professors with expertise in this area and technology support personnel were invited. Several issues came up during the ensuing discussion. In the end, everyone agreed that distance learning (its implications as well as its potential) was a strategic issue needing to be addressed, and that a comprehensive evaluation was required, but one that could be completed within a relatively short period of time. The decision was made to hire the services of Resurgo, Inc, a firm that specializes in information technology strategies for education and training.

The lead analyst on this project is Dr. Anne Galway. Dr. Galway met with several faculty, staff, students , and administrators over a 3-week period. She then conducted some additional research on the competitive position of Optima in the institutions of higher learning market. Her findings on the strategic analysis of distance learning for Optima University are summarized below.

a. Is there a true business need for distance learning at Optima University? Optima would potentially see an increase in new revenues from implementing distance learning for the following two reasons:

- There would be an increased reach to new populations of students. The three immediate markets she saw include interested alumni who cannot take courses at Optima right now because of geographical limitations; new students around the country that would be interested in Optima's distance learning courses; and existing students who could take additional courses in the summer that they cannot right now because of their summer employment.
- Increased net revenues could be expected from lower delivery costs associated with distance learning. These would happen because delivery costs would be minimal if the courses were Web-based and student-to-instructor ratios could be increased. To maintain Optima's quality interaction between faculty and students, computer-mediated collaborative tools would be required to support the Web-based instructional content. The

conversion of already existing instructional content would be relatively inexpensive given advanced course development tools on the market today.

In addition, Dr. Galway determined that distance learning could provide some strategic advantages for Optima University using two specific strategies:

- Total conversion of popular courses taught by nationally recognized scholars that graduates and other students across the country would seek to participate in.
- Technology insertion and partial conversion of resident courses where enrollment was high, traditional classes were large, and courses were given in the lecture-based format.

b. Who are the major stakeholders of this project, and who would be its champion? The major stakeholders (affected by distance learning) at Optima University include the Board of Regents, students, faculty, and support personnel. The Board of Regents oversees quality issues in education, and must ensure that distance learning will not negatively impact this quality. Faculty will be required to participate actively in the distance learning initiative, and impacts on their research and teaching productivity must be evaluated. Current and potential students may have to adapt to this changed way that learning would be delivered to them. Support personnel will be required to provide technical support to a greater number of students and faculty when they go on-line, and adequate support infrastructures, including technology and personnel must be planned.

Dr. Galway also discussed the leadership role in the distance learning project with several stakeholders. She recommends that the Dean of the Engineering school, Dr. Farmer, who is a particularly strong advocate of the potential of distance learning and has indicated his interest in this responsibility, be appointed to lead its implementation.

c.   What were the time and funding restrictions for the DL conversion project? The Board of Regents is interested in funding only a small experiment in distance learning, and they want to start the project during the current fiscal year. They would evaluate its effect and its financial results, and make decisions during next year's budget programming on whether to expand the program. They agreed to fund a strategic analysis and project plan, with a pilot implementation of no more than three courses to start.

d. What are the goals and objectives of the courses to be converted? Before identifying the courses that would be part of the pilot implementation, Dr. Galway started contacting alumni to find out what types of post-graduate learning experiences they were involved in, both degree and non-degree granting, how much time they spent in these learning experiences, what types of learning activities comprised the courses, and what they paid. She then completed a similar survey on the freshman seminars. After looking at the revenue potential for the courses reported in the survey, two types of courses were found to have the most potential for offering distance learning delivery:

1) Introductory level MBA coursework that can be taken towards the MBA degree.
2) Other non-degree granting courses (e.g., art, philosophy, history, computer science) taught by nationally recognized scholars in the field.

Dr. Galway recommended that selection of the three courses for the implementation pilot should be done among these two categories of courses.

e. How to evaluate these courses for DL suitability ? The preliminary course information forms (from Appendix A) were filled out and analyzed (see below for an example of a history course). Of the 36 potential courses surveyed, five introductory MBA courses showed the most promise for total conversion, and two introductory courses (one in history and one by a Nobel laureate in genetic engineering) in non-degree granting fields also showed promise for total conversion. For example, the Introduction to History course for which forms A-1 and A-2 are filled, has great potential for distance learning since it obtained 8 points on form A-2 and has a high student throughput of 800 students per year, as calculated on form A-1. All of the freshman seminars could be accommodated at the same time, despite

Table 7-1. Course Information Form

Course ID	HIS 2104
Course Name	Introduction to History
Instructor's name	Paul Smith, John Markham, Mary Jones
Instructor POC info	History Dept. 555.555.2135
Course frequency per year	8
Length of course (instructional hours)	45
Average class size	100
Learner throughput	800 / year

Table 7-2. Course DL Screening Form

Add up the "yes" and "no" points in each column. Add them together and use the resulting number to interpret as follows:

0, negative values=DL is not suitable
1-3=DL may not be suitable; consider using technology insertion
4-6=Consider combined delivery
7+=DL is highly suitable

Course ID:

VARIABLE	Yes -1	No +1
Hands-on activities essential	No +1	
Specialized tools or equipment is required	No +1	
Group training in functional teams is required	No +1	
Group problem solving is required	No +1	
Continuous feedback from instructor required	No +1	
Instructor-guided discussion required	No +1	
Group discussions are conducted	No +1	
Other requirement for physical presence of instructor and student	No +1	
Learner performance data required	Yes -1	
Learning objectives involve physical risk to student [reverse code: yes=1, no= -1]	No +1	

the sharp increase in freshman enrollment, if they were partially conducted in a distance learning mode. The instructors could accommodate more students simultaneously by meeting with each seminar once every two weeks, and having students engage in a variety of collaborative exchanges through asynchronous threaded discussions, synchronous chat sessions, and email.

f. What will be the ROI? Once Dr. Galway had determined that distance learning would be a valuable endeavor for Optima University, she calculated rough estimates of return on investment potential for distance learning initiatives at Optima. She didn't take into consideration the three pilot implementation courses into her calculation. Nevertheless, her analysis indicated that the following investments would have to be made for converting and implementing 15 courses to distance learning formats for the next three years:

1) Total equipment costs (server, peripherals, and additional network connections) and Software (including a Course Management System): $ 1,050,000

2) Total courseware development costs (at $3,000,000 per year): $9,000,000

3) Personnel (development and support over three years at $ 250,000 per year): $ 750,000.

Assuming that five courses are converted and ready for delivery each year, the costs and anticipated revenues were calculated as presented in Table 7-3.

As the chart indicates, the distance learning program will begin to return on its investment by the third year.

The ROI over three years is calculated as:

$$\frac{12,500,000 - 10,800,000}{10,800,000} = 15.7\%$$

Table 7-3. ROI Estimates for Optima University

	Year 1	Year 2	Year 3
Total courses converted that year	5	5	5
Total aggregate courses delivered by DL	5	10	15
Costs of equipment, infrastructure upgrades	$ 450,000	$ 25,000	$ 25,000
Cost of course management system (virtual campus application software), yearly license	$ 250,000	$ 150,000	$ 150,000
Course development costs*	$ 3,000,000	$ 3,000,000	$ 3,000,000
Support personnel salaries	$ 250,000	$ 250,000	$ 250,000
Total cost per year	$ 3,950,000	$ 3,425,000	$ 3,425,000
CUMULATIVE COSTS	$ 3,950,000	$ 7,375,000	$10,800,000
DL Student throughput (cumulative) per year based on anticipated virtual enrollment	3,500	7,000	12,500
Revenue per student (cumulative) @ average of $1,000 per student	$ 3,500,000	$ 7,000,000	$12,500,000
NET	$ (450,000)	$ (375,000)	$ 1,700,000
Cumulative	$ (450,000)	$ (825,000)	$ 875,000

*Assumes existing course design and course content, some graphics, videos, and other multimedia files used in the classroom by professors and that professors design the content of their own courses.

CASE STUDY II: COURSE CONVERSION ANALYSIS

Caretaker Insurance

Background

Caretaker Insurance is a medium-sized company based in the southwest. Its founder was an early advocate of information technology, and by the early 1990's the company had established a back office operation in Florida where most of its claims processing was automated. By the mid-90's, telephone operators for the company who handled incoming calls from policy holders were able to forward both the call and the database record to the agent handling the call-this eliminated the need for the policy holder to repeat his/her name, policy number, and reason for the call each time he/she was transferred to an agent. This was the beginning of a large integration of "front office" (client service activities) with traditional "back office" (policy administration, claims adjustments, event reporting) activities.

In the past year, the company has become fully automated so that every transaction, from initial marketing call to policy creation, policy adjustments, claim reporting and processing is fully accessible and viewable by the agent "on site" with the client. Agents take a laptop with wireless communication devices with them to the client's home, scene of accident, or workplace. From there, they can open up a new policy, access company demographic and customer profiles to determine rates and coverage. They can report events (accidents, death, or external claims against the insured) online to the company's database via a secure Web-based interface, and can submit a claims transaction from their laptop that is validated automatically using expert systems algorithms at their company's processing headquarters, and audited online by designated company auditors. Whereas these transactions took days and sometimes more than a week to process previously, most routine processing is accomplished within four hours under this automated processing.

Training at Caretaker

While the new collaborative, integrated system, called "Patriot", is both effective and efficient, the company's biggest problem turned out to be training. Its training department has outsourced all training to a small firm called Just-in-Time Training that was located near its southwest headquarters. Bob Burke, the training manager, was frustrated by JITT's seeming lack of initiative in developing new training materials for the Agent-in-the-Field course, which combined some of the knowledge-based tasks that was in the Policy Processing course with the Customer Servicing course that agents previously took. Under the training agreement, Caretaker's subject matter experts (mid-level managers and information technology experts) designed and developed the course content for JITT, who then created presentation materials for the classroom and delivered stand-up training at their JITT building.

Before the new Patriot system was implemented, Caretaker sent approximately 750 of its agents to JITT each year for the Total Customer Servicing course, and approximately 350 of its back office administrative workers to its Policy Processing course. Each course was four days long, with a half day of travel time each way. Since the back office was located in Florida, these employees were away from their home office for a week, and the cost of airfare, hotel, and food was approximately $1,300 per student. The value of the employee's 40-hours of labor was averaged out to be $700. The agents flew in to JITT from all over the 50 states, but most were located in the southwest, southeast, and along the Mid-Atlantic. The average cost of airfare, hotel, and food for these agents was $1,900, and the value of their 40-hours of labor for the week was averaged out to be $1300. The content of the new course was such that the newly developed Caretaker course was seven days in length, which means that agents had to stay over the weekend, where they participated in simulated casework with role-playing experts from Caretaker acting out the parts of accident claimants, police officers, and other information providers that they would be expected to interact with to process their claims. Given that the course length has increased to 56 hours, and that the size of the class must be smaller because of the interactive activities and the need for workstations for each student, JITT has told the training manager that an additional classroom would have to be installed, with an increased cost-per-student for training.

Evaluating Distance Learning at Caretaker

Is distance learning delivery of any one or all three of these courses a viable alternative? Based on the instructional characteristics of the

Table 7-4a. Policy Processing: Course Information Form

Course ID	PP-01
Course Name	Policy Processing
Instructor's name	Susan Burns, John Smith
Instructor POC info	555.212.2222
Course frequency per year	20
Length of course (instructional hours)	40
Average class size	15-20
Learner throughput	350 / year

Table 7-4b. Policy Processing: Course Dl Screening Form

Add up the "yes" and "no" points in each column. Add them together and use the resulting number to interpret as follows:

0, negative values=DL is not suitable
1-3=DL may not be suitable; consider using technology insertion
4-6=Consider combined delivery
7+=DL is highly suitable

Course ID:	PP-01
VARIABLE	**Yes -1 No +1**
Hands-on activities essential	Yes -1
Specialized tools or equipment is required	No +1
Group training in functional teams is required	No +1
Group problem solving is required	No +1
Continuous feedback from instructor required	No +1
Instructor-guided discussion required	No +1
Group discussions are conducted	No +1
Other requirement for physical presence of instructor and student	No +1
Learner performance data required	Yes -1
Learning objectives involve physical risk to student	No +1

Policy Processing course, it is suitable for conversion to a distance learning format.

The Policy Processing course involves mostly stand-up lecture with some question and answer interactions with the teacher, and there are two units involving computer-based learning activities. Based on the types of learning objectives and how these objectives are assessed, the Policy Processing course would be suitable for a Web-based delivery with support from computer-mediated communication technologies for learner-instructor interaction. The computer-based exercises might be suitable for a standalone CD-ROM delivery

Table 7-4c. Policy Processing: Instructional Unit Form

List all instructional units in the course, with the following information.

Course ID: PP-01

Instructional Unit	# of hours	Instructional activities [1]	Type of learning objective[2]	How objective assessed [3]	Media choices[4]
1	8	1	1	N/a	2,4
2	8	1,2	1	N/a	2,4,5
3	8	1,2	3	1,2,3	2,3
4	8	6	2	N/a	1,2
5	8	6	2	N/a	1,2

Instructional unit: a group of lessons or modules that are integrated to complete a usable skill, knowledge, or to aid in scheduling a course. An instructional unit is a basic component of courses, and when developed or converted into a learning module for DL delivery. It is the basic unit of reuse that can be combined, integrated, or re-scheduled in a course.

[1]**Instructional activities:**
1=lecture
2=question & answer
3=instructor demo
4=instructor-guided discussions
5=student group activity
6=hands-on activity

[2]**Learning objective types:**
1=Cognitive
2= Software
3=Problem solving
4=Affective
5=Psychomotor

[3]**Assessment types:**
1=multiple choice
2=fill-in-blanks
3=short answer
4=essay questions
5=topical/research paper
6= individual project
7=oral presentation
8=group project

[4]**Appropriate media choices:**

1=CBT/CAI
2=WBT
3=TC
4=VTT or videotape
5=CBT/WBT

of instruction.

Although most of the activities in the Customer Servicing course make it suitable for distance learning conversion, there are group problem solving activities, instructor-guided discussions, and group discussions. These types of activities suggest that a combined delivery of standup lecture, distance learning, and computer-based training may be appropriate. An alternative possibility is to use collaboration tools to support the group interactivity and communication. The net benefit of a shorter period of resident training is that while airline costs

Table 7-5a. Customer Servicing: Course Information Form

Course ID	CS-01
Course Name	Customer Servicing
Instructor's name	Robert Aveeda, Cindy Small
Instructor POC info	555.212.8818
Course frequency per year	35
Length of course (instructional hrs)	40
Average class size	20-25
Learner throughput	750

Table 7-5b. Customer Servicing: Course DL Screening Form

Add up the "yes" and "no" points in each column. Add them together and use the resulting number to interpret as follows:

0, negative values=DL is not suitable
1-3=DL may not be suitable; consider using technology insertion
4-6=Consider combined delivery
7+=DL is highly suitable

Course ID:	CS-01
VARIABLE	Yes -1 No +1
Hands-on activities essential	No +1
Specialized tools or equipment is required	No +1
Group training in functional teams is required	No +1
Group problem solving is required	Yes -1
Continuous feedback from instructor required	No +1
Instructor-guided discussion required	Yes -1
Group discussions are conducted	Yes -1
Other requirement for physical presence of instructor and student	No +1
Learner performance data required	Yes -1
Learning objectives involve physical risk to student	No +1

are still required, the per diem (hotel, food, car) costs would be reduced.

There are three distinct types of classroom activities in this course. Three of the units of the course are traditional standup lectures with question-and-answer interaction with the instructor, with the last of these three involving instructor demo. Two units involve computer-based exercises, and the final two units involve group interaction, role playing, and the completion of a short topical paper. A hybrid delivery strategy that combines Web-based training with standalone CD ROM computer-based training, and the use of computer-medi-

Table 7-5c. Customer Servicing: Instructional Unit Form

List all instructional units in the course, with the following information.

Course ID: CS-01

Instructional Unit	# of hours	Instructional activities [1]	Type of learning objective[2]	How objective assessed [3]	Media choices[4]
1	8	1,2	1	N/a	2
2	8	1,2	1	N/a	2
3	8	1,2,3	3	N/a	2+3
4	8	6	2,6	1,2,3,4	1,2,5
5	8	6	2,6	6	1,2,5
6	8	1,2,4,5	1,3	6	3+4,2+3
7	8	1,2,4,5	1,3	7	3+4,2+3

Instructional unit: a group of lessons or modules that are integrated to complete a usable skill, knowledge, or to aid in scheduling a course. An instructional unit is a basic component of courses, and when developed or converted into a learning module for DL delivery. It is the basic unit of reuse that can be combined, integrated, or re-scheduled in a course.

[1]**Instructional activities:**
1=lecture
2=question & answer
3=instructor demo
4=instructor-guided discussions
5=student group activity
6=hands-on activity

[2]**Learning objective types:**
1=Cognitive
2= Software
3=Problem solving
4=Affective
5=Psychomotor

[3]**Assessment types:**
1=multiple choice
2=fill-in-blanks
3=short answer
4=essay questions
5=topical/research paper
6= individual project
7=oral presentation
8=group project

[4]**Appropriate media choices:**
1=CBT/CAI
2=WBT
3=TC
4=VTT or videotape
5=CBT/WBT

ated collaborative tools to support group interaction and facilitate group discussions is recommended.

There are several activities in this course that suggest that either a partial conversion is suitable, or a delivery method that uses computer-mediated collaboration tools. This course has all the high-communication requirements that the Customer Servicing course has, because it uses the same course content for that portion of the curricu-

Table 7-6a. Caretaker: Course Information Form

Course ID	CT-00
Course Name	Caretaker Introduction
Instructor's name	Robert Aveeda, Susan Burns
Instructor POC info	555.212.5555
Course frequency per year	37
Length of course (instructional hours)	56
Average class size	15-20
Learner throughput	750

Table 7-6b. Caretaker: Course DL Screening Form

Add up the "yes" and "no" points in each column. Add them together and use the resulting number to interpret as follows:

0, negative values=DL is not suitable
1-3=DL may not be suitable; consider using technology insertion
4-6=Consider combined delivery
7+=DL is highly suitable

Course ID:	CT-00
VARIABLE	**Yes -1 No +1**
Hands-on activities essential	Yes -1
Specialized tools or equipment is required	No +1
Group training in functional teams is required	No +1
Group problem solving is required	Yes -1
Continuous feedback from instructor required	No +1
Instructor-guided discussion required	Yes -1
Group discussions are conducted	Yes -1
Other requirement for physical presence of instructor and student	No +1
Learner performance data required	Yes -1
Learning objectives involve physical risk to student	No +1

lum from the Customer Servicing course.

From an instructional design perspective, this course has redundant content with the previous two courses, the Customer Servicing course and the Policy Processing course. The redundant content of the course could be developed into learning modules (from each of the previous two courses), and then reused for this course, for considerable savings in course development costs. These reusable learning objects should also be evaluated for potential inclusion in other training courses.

Similar to the Customer Servicing course, a hybrid delivery strategy using shareable courseware objects, is suggested for this

Table 7-6c. Caretaker: Instructional Unit Form

List all instructional units in the course, with the following information.

Course ID: CT-00

Instructional Unit	# of hours	Instructional activities [1]	Type of learning objective[2]	How objective assessed [3]	Media choices[4]
1	8	1,2,4	1	N/a	2
2	8	1,2,4	1	N/a	2
3	8	1,2,4,5	3	N/a	2+3
4	8	6	2,6	1,2,3,4	1,2,5
5	8	6	2,6	6	1,2,5
6	8	1,2,4,5	1,3	6	3+4,2+3
7	8	1,2,4,5	1,3	7	3+4,2+3

Instructional unit: a group of lessons or modules that are integrated to complete a usable skill, knowledge, or to aid in scheduling a course. An instructional unit is a basic component of courses, and when developed or converted into a learning module for DL delivery. It is the basic unit of reuse that can be combined, integrated, or re-scheduled in a course.

[1]**Instructional activities:**
1=lecture
2=question & answer
3=instructor demo
4=instructor-guided discussions
5=student group activity
6=hands-on activity

[2]**Learning objective types:**
1=Cognitive
2= Software
3=Problem solving
4=Affective
5=Psychomotor

[3]**Assessment types:**
1=multiple choice
2=fill-in-blanks
3=short answer
4=essay questions
5=topical/research paper
6= individual project
7=oral presentation
8=group project

[4]**Appropriate media choices:**
1=CBT/CAI
2=WBT
3=TC
4=VTT or videotape
5=CBT/WBT

course. The hybrid strategy would include Web-based delivery, standalone computer-based training on CD-ROM, and the use of computer-mediated collaboration tools.

CASE STUDY III: INFRASTRUCTURE ANALYSIS

Teknica Solutions

Background

Teknica Solutions is a large information technology organization specializing in providing client/server solutions to customers. It has a long list of products, including hardware and software, for sale in its national and international offices. Branding itself as a "total solutions" vendor, Teknica also offers both fixed priced and time & materials programming and consulting services to its customers.

Teknica was founded more than 30 years ago by a visionary, Albert Syms, and has evolved from a mainframe vendor to today's total client/server solutions provider. The current president of the corporation, Robert Anderson, was appointed by the Executive Committee four years ago in an attempt to regain rapidly decreasing market share of the lucrative information systems market. While Teknica's main offices are located in the northeastern United States, the core of its business is run by regional vice-presidents who each have several offices in most of the major cities across the U.S. Its international operations include offices in more than 20 countries in Europe, South America, Africa, and Asia.

Anyone in the corporation would confirm President Anderson's statements that marketing and sales are the core of the business at Teknica, even though the production environments are required to produce leading edge and competitive products on the market. The company prides itself on achieving superior relationships with its customers, who constantly rate Teknica as one of the leading information technology organizations among its many global competitors.

Training at Teknica

Training has always been a key element in Teknica's personnel policies. New hires receive extensive training on the company's products and services. Every year, each employee receives at least two weeks of refresher training because the company considers that the knowledge base of its employees is a competitive advantage. Technical courses available to Teknica employees include technology overviews of the company's products, industry trends, and competitors' products and marketing strategies. A true-believer, as well as practitioner in the concept of the learning organization, Teknica's leaders offer all employees additional training opportunities in addition to their required two weeks of internal training each year.

In recent years, Teknica has been faced with the constant challenge of reducing the cycle time of bringing their new products to market in an increasingly competitive global environment. When President Anderson met with senior executives at a retreat to discuss these issues, several vice-presidents suggested that they could no longer afford to let new hires attend training sessions for the first four months on the job. They also mentioned that requiring employees to travel to training sites at least two weeks a year has a tremendous impact on the overall productivity levels, particularly when you take into account that Teknica has more than 10,000 employees in the U.S. alone. At the same time, everyone agrees that it is impossible to cut training as Teknica would be creating major handicaps for the future of its workforce. Recent developments in technologies led President Anderson and several of his senior managers to recommend distance learning as a way to achieve the best of both worlds: an educated work force that retains high levels of productivity by limiting travel and training time.

Distance Learning at Teknica

Some forms of distance learning courses have existed at Teknica for a long time. For example, videotapes were produced on high-interest and high-value topics and made available to each local office. They were used in some of the new hire orientation and training sessions. Because its core competency is in advanced information technologies, Teknica installed large-scale video conferencing facilities in most of its large offices. In addition, over the past 10 years, Teknica implemented an extensive virtual private communications network between its offices for electronic data interchange, electronic messaging, and distributed computer applications.

President Anderson has assigned a task force composed of employees and middle managers under the supervision of the Senior Vice President for Human Resources, Joanne Bickson, to identify better ways to offer distance learning alternatives to its employees. He particularly highlighted the following objectives:

- Teknica must continue to be a learning organization that offers extensive training opportunities to all of its employees.
- Teknica should leverage its existing and vast communication networks and facilities around the world.
- Teknica should try to significantly lower the amount of travel required for employees to attend/take training.
- Teknica's training department must ensure that the quality of training and learning is the same or better than that of current courses offered in traditional classroom environments.
- Teknica must find distance learning alternatives that could be implemented in the international offices as well as offices throughout the U.S.

The task force met several times over a two-month period and established several guidelines. They also assigned one individual, Paul Crammer, with full-time responsibility in evaluating distance learning alternatives for this organization. Since the corporation offers currently more than 500 courses, it was decided that course screening forms would be completed (Appendix A) for groups of courses and individual courses where appropriate. Paul Crammer spent numerous hours gathering information and filling out the forms. The preliminary results of this analysis were then presented by Joanne Bickson to the President and the Executive Committee. The major findings are summarized below.

- Best candidate courses for distance learning: company product training.
- Worst candidate courses for distance learning: company competitive information courses.
- Characteristics of the company product courses.
  a. Company product courses provide technical information on the products of the company. These include non-competitive information by nature and shouldn't create any security concerns.
  b. Given that the products can change on average once a year (improvements, new versions, fixes, etc.), the courses have to be easily changeable. That is the main reason why the courses were never offered on videotape in the first place.
  c. In addition, several of these courses benefit from some hands-on practice by learners. Therefore, any kind of interactive

medium for course delivery would increase quality of the training provided to employees.

- Finally, given that these courses represent the largest portion of all courses offered by the company (300+), an investment in offering company product training courses via distance learning would prove quite economically beneficial in the long run.

The president was pleased to see that a large number of courses could be converted to distance learning and that there were some substantial economic benefits that could be expected. He asked the committee to proceed further and evaluate the best distance learning alternative for these courses. Joanne Bickson requested a technical support person to perform the analysis. This analyst then decided that the best starting point for evaluating distance learning initiatives would be to analyze the corporations' technical infrastructure using the forms in Appendix C. Table 7-7 presents this analysis.

Following the analysis of the infrastructure, it became apparent to Paul Crammer that different courses would be better served by using different distance learning alternatives. However, he also noticed that most of the technology courses on the corporation's products were already partly produced on some forms of video streams for customer demonstrations. He therefore concluded that using a distance learning delivery mechanism that allowed videos to be used would provide substantial benefits in reduced course preparation time. Given the existing infrastructure of the corporation, which includes an extensive and reliable high bandwidth network and desktop workstations on every employee's desk, the analyst recommended the use of desktop video conferencing for several of these courses. The company hired outside education specialists to develop the courses, which are now offered upon request directly at each employee's work desk.

Table 7-7. Infrastructure Survey and Upgrade Requirements

INTERNET REQUIREMENTS Internet connectivity? • Asynchronous capability • Synchronous capability	**Instructor/learner upgrades required** 100% Internet connectivity for all employees. Large bandwidth pipes (OC-3 or greater). Fast Etherswitch LANs w/10Mbs dedicated capacity to each workstation.
• How accessible is this connectivity?	Always available.
How will connectivity be achieved? • Modem /dial up • LAN • WAN	Department LAN in the office environment. DSL, ISDN, and dialup modem connectivity at V.90 (56kbs or greater) for remote users.
• How fast is the speed of connectivity?	Minimum 56 Kb for dialup. 10Mbs dedicated for each work-station at work.
Is Internet connectivity provided through a shared facility?	Shared LAN but dedicated bandwidth for each workstation.
Do you have an Internet E-mail account?	All instructors and learners have corporate Internet E-mail account.
DESKTOP/LAN	**Instructor upgrades required**
Is your desktop connected to an LAN?	Yes, with remote dialup connectivity on a virtual private network.
Do you have access to a shared file server?	Yes, by department or work group.
Do you have a web browser loaded on your desktop?	All PCs have a standard browser loaded for use.
Are web plug-ins allowed on your workstation? • Java • Shockwave • Adobe Acrobat • Real Audio	Plug-ins are available for download from the corporate Intranet site.
What office productivity software do you have access to? • Lotus Suite • Microsoft Office	Lotus Suite and Microsoft Office are both available and supported through corporate licenses.

What graphics packages do you use?	All of the most commercially popular graphics packages are supported and licensed by the firm.
What type of desktop hardware do you have? • 486 (<150 Mhz) • Pentium I (150-300 Mhz) • Pentium II (300+ Mhz)	Standard desktop is the Pentium III, which has just been released.
What is the storage capacity of your desktop? • <5 Gb • 5 or more Gb	All desktops have at least 6 Gb of storage, with over 50% having at least 10 Gb. Corporate laptops have 2-6 Gb of storage but employees can order upgrades.
Is your desktop equipped with multimedia capability? • Sound card • Speakers • Color monitor that can display 16 bit (256) colors • Video card • Video camera • Microphone	Each corporate desktop is fully equipped for multimedia, including desktop VTC equipment. The company has just installed VTC to the desktop capability.
What desktop operating system(s) do you use? • Windows 3.1 or 95/98 • OS/2 • Macintosh • Linux • Unix	Over 50% use Windows 98; the remaining 50% use Windows 95 and expect to move to Windows 2000. Corporate web servers include NT and UNIX machines.
What network operation system do you use? • Novell • Windows NT • Other	Most shared applications and communication tools in the company are designed for a Windows platform, except for some web-based applications that are on UNIX.
E-mail platform(s) • MS Mail • Lotus Notes • Microsoft Exchange • CcMail • Netscape Messenger	E-Mail capability required to support DL includes sending and receiving attachments and multimedia files; ability to participate in listservers and newsgroups; ability to send/ receive large files.

Do you have an Intranet (web-based access to corporate LAN and applications) in your organization?	Although not required, organizations with an Intranet can create a thriving learning environment that is easily accessible (at high speed) to all employees when they are at work. The Intranet can also be access by remote dialup if employees have an account.
What is aggregate throughput of data on LAN?	Fast Etherswitch of 400+Mbs with dedicated10Mbsto each desktop.
What is protocol of LAN? • TCP/IP • Novell Netware • Microsoft NT domain	TCP/IP supported on Novell Netware.
COLLABORATION	**Instructor upgrades required**
Do you have access to collaboration user software? • Shared whiteboard • NetMeeting • Listservs • Web forum • [others]	All web-based collaborative applications are supported (web forums-both threaded and synchronous chats), VTC over IP using NetMeeting, shared whiteboards, and internal listservers, and group decision support software.
Do you have a server dedicated to host collaboration software?	There are four dedicated servers to host collaboration software.
USER SUPPORT	
Are you supported by a Help Desk?	A 24x7 virtual Help Desk (phone, email, fax, and web-based applications) is available to all employees around the world.
How quick is the response time when you call for help? • <one hour • 1-3 hours • 4-8 hours • l-2 days • >2 days	A "triage" system for help categories the type of trouble call, with calls fielded to the technical group that is most likely to provide a quick and effective solution. Help Desk support applications keep track of all calls, and statistical analyses are available to track tickets. An internal knowledge management system has been added to capture "lessons learned" and provide remedial training or updated training for technical problems/solutions.

Is the Help Desk staffed around the clock?	7x24 coverage, worldwide, in English, Spanish, and French.
VIDEO TELECONFERENCING	
Type of TC system	The corporation has both large scale and desktop videoconferencing systems. Large scale systems are installed in each main office. The large scale systems are installed in conference rooms with a maximum of 10 participants. The desktop facilities are provided using a video conferencing software package developed internally that can be easily installed on each employee's workstation.
How many hours per month is allocated for TC training?	In large scale facilities, no time is currently allocated for training.
Studio capacity (student seats)	Ten
VIDEO/INTERACTIVE TV	
Do you have access to a broadcast facility?	No
How many broadcast studios do you have access to?	N/A
Do you have access to downlink facilities?	Yes, but located within the teleconferencing rooms described above.
How many classrooms have VTT reception capability?	N/A
How many hours per month are available for VTT or video programming?	N/A
What types of support personnel are available for the VTT uplink and downlink facilities?	N/A
Does your uplink site have the ability to connect with desktops?	N/A
Is there a video library in your organization?	Yes. Several videotapes were produced in-house and several others were acquired on the market. Videotapes, however, tend to be out-dated.

COMPUTER LEARNING CENTER/LAB	
Do you have access to a computer learning center/lab?	LCs are fully equipped with multimedia workstations for CBT learning; labs are equipped with synchronous communication tools for TC as well.
How many computers are installed in the lab?	Each lab has 20-35 workstations. Each regional office has at least one lab.
What is the student to computer ratio for lab use? • 1-2 students per computer • 2-5 students per computer • 6-10 students per computer • 11-20 students per computer • 21+ students per computer	The ratio of students to computer lab is somewhat high (50 students per computer), but most students elect to do their training at their own workstations or at home. Only certain specialized courses require students' presence in the computer lab.

Bibliography
and
References

Alavi, M.; Wheeler, B. C. & Valacich, J. S.   (1995).   Using IT to Reengineer Business Education: An Exploratory Investigation of Collaborative Telelearning. *MIS Quarterly*, 19(3), 293-312.

Bateman, D. & Simpson, V. (1995).   Hypertext in The Classroom: Changing the Roles of Teacher and Students. In F. Percival, R. Land, & D. Edgar-Nevill (Eds.), *Computer Assisted and Open Access Education*. London: Kogan Page Ltd.

Berlo, D.K. (1960). *The Process of Communication: An Introduction to Theory and Practice*. New York: Holt, Rinehart, and Winston.

Bloom, B. S. (Ed.). (1956). *Taxonomy of Educational Objectives, Book 1: Cognitive Domain*. New York: Longman.

Bonime, A. & Pohlman, K. C. (1998). *Writing for New Media: The Essential Guide to Writing for Interactive Media, CD-ROMs, and the Web*. New York: John Wiley & Sons.

Clark, R.E. (1994). Assessment of Distance Learning Technology. In E.L. Baker & F.O. Harold (Eds.), *Technology Assessment in Education and Training*, Hillsdale, NJ: Erlbaum.

Daft, R. L. & Lengel, R. H. (1986). A Proposed Integration Among Organizational Requirements, Media Richness, and Structural Design. *Management Science*,32, 554-571.

Darby, J. (1992). Computers in Teaching and Learning in U.K. *Higher Education. Computers and Education*, 19(1/2), 1-8.

Dobson, R. (1995). The Case for Flexible Learning. In F. Percival, R. Land, & D. Edgar-Nevill (Eds.), *Computer Assisted and Open Access Education*, London: Kogan Page.

Ellington, H. (1995). Flexible Learning, Your Flexible Friend. In C. Bell., M. Bowden & A. Trott. (Eds.), *Implementing Flexible Learning*, London: Kogan Page.

Encarta® 98 Encyclopedia, Microsoft Corporation, 1993-1997.

Farance, F. & Tonkel, J.. (1998). Learning Technology Systems Architecture. (Version 4.0), Farance, Inc.

Firman, K. (1995). The Development of A Computer-Based Teaching System Based on the Toolbook Programming Software. In F. Percival, R. Land & D. Edgar-Nevill. (Eds.), *Computer Assisted and Open Access Education*, London: Kogan Page.

Frenza, J. P. & Szabo, M. (1996). *Web & New Media Pricing Guide*. Indianapolis: Hayden Books.

Gardner, H. (1993). *Frames of Mind: The Theory of Multiple Intelligences*. New York: Basic Books.

Gubernick, L. & Ebeling, A. (1997). I Got My Degree Through E-mail. *Forbes*, 159(12), 84-92.

Hall, B. (1997) *Web-based Training Cookbook*. New York: John Wiley & Sons.

Hiltz, S. R. (1997). Asynchronous Learning Networks as a Virtual Classroom. *Communication of the ACM*, 40(9), 44-49.

Ivers, K. S. & Barron, A. E. (1998). *Multimedia Projects in Education*. Englewood: Teachers Idea Press.

Jonassen, D. H. (1993). Thinking Technology. *Educational Technology*, January, 35-37.

Kirkpatrick, D. L. (1994). *Evaluation Training Programs: The Four Levels*. San Francisco: Berrett-Kohler.

Krathwohl, D. R., Bloom, B. S., & Masia, B. B. (1964). *Taxonomy of Educational Objectives, Book 2: Affective Domain*. New York: Longman.

Kulik, J. M. (1994). Meta-Analytic Findings on Computer-Based Instruction. In E.L. Baker & F.O. Harold. (Eds.). *Technology Assessment in Education and Training*. Hillsdale: Erlbaum.

Landon, B. http://www.ctt.bc.ca/landonline/glossary.html, 1998.

Landon, B. http://www.ctt.bc.ca/landonline/choices.html, 1998.

LaRose, R., Gregg, J. & Eastin, M. (1998) Audiographic Telecourses for the Web: An Experiment. *Journal of Computer Mediated Communication*, 4(2).

Leidner, D. E. & Jarvenpaa, S. L. (1995). The use of Information Technology to Enhance Management School Education: A

Theoretical View. *MIS Quarterly*, 19(3), 265-291.

Mantyla, K. & Gividen, J. R. (1997). *Distance Learning: A Step-by-Step Guide for Trainers*. Alexandria, VA: American Society for Training & Development.

McArdle, G. E. (1999). *Training Design and Delivery*. Alexandria, VA: American Society for Training & Development.

McCormack, C. & Jones, D. (1997). *Building a Web-based Education System*. New York: John Wiley & Sons.

MIL-HDBK-1379-3, *Department of Defense Handbook* (1997). Development of Interactive Multimedia Instruction.

Moore, M. (1973). Towards a Theory of Independent Learning and Teaching. *Journal of Higher Education*, 44, 666-678.

National Center for Educational Statistics report, October 1997, http://nces.ed.gov/.

Phillips, J. J. (1994). (Ed.). *Measuring Return on Investment: Volume I.* Alexandria, VA: American Society for Training & Development.

Phillips, J. J. (1997). (Ed.) *Measuring Return on Investment: Volume II.* Alexandria, VA; American Society for Training & Development.

Race, P. & Brown, S. (1995). Getting the Word Right. In F. Percival, R. Land & D. Edgar-Nevill. (Eds.). *Computer Assisted and Open Access Education*. London: Kogan Page.

Russell, T. L. (1996). The No Significant Difference Phenomenon. http://cuda.teleeducation.nb.ca/nosignificantdifference/.

Scotney, B. & McClean, S. (1995). The Design and Use of Computer-Based Tutorials for Teaching. *Learning and Assessment of Quantitative Research Methods*, 80-86.

Schaff, D. (1997). A Pipeline Full of Promises: Distance Training is Ready to Deliver. *Training*, 34(10), A6-A12.

Shannon, C. E. (1948). A Mathematical Theory of Communication. *Bell Systems Technical Journal*, 27(3), 379-423.

Slavin, R.E. (1990). *Cooperative Learning: Theory, Research, and Practice*. Englewood Cliffs, NJ: Prentice Hall.

Stanton, N. & Stammers, R. (1990). A Comparison of Structured and Unstructured Navigation through a CBT Package. *Computers and Education*, 15(1-3), 159-163.

Tannenbaum, R. S. (1998). *Theoretical Foundations of Multimedia*. New York: Computer Science Press.

Taylor, C. D. & Burnkrant, S. R. (1998). Virginia Tech On-Line Summer School 1998 Assessment Report, http://www.edtech.vt.edu/assess/ol_summer98.

UNESCO. (1987). *Distance Learning Systems and Structures: Training Manual, Report of a Sub-Regional Training Workshop, Vol. II.* Bangkok.

Van Slyke, C., Kittner, M. & Belanger, F. (1998). Identifying Candidates for Distance Education: A Telecommuting Perspective. *Proceedings of the America's Conference on Information Systems.* Baltimore, 666-668.

Villamil-Casanova J. & Molina, L. (1997). *Multimedia: An Introduction.* Indianapolis: MacMillan.

Waagen, A. K. (1998). Essentials for Evaluation. InfoLine, Issue 9705. In *Instructional Systems Development.* Alexandria, VA: American Society for Training & Development, 237-252.

Walther, J. B. "Interpersonal Effects in Computer Mediated Interaction: A Relational Perspective," *Communication Research* (19), 1992, 52-90.

Walther, J. B. (1995). Relational Aspects of Computer-Mediated Communication: Experimental Observations Over Time. *Organization Science*, 6(2), 186-203.

Webster, J. & Hackley, P. (1997).. Teaching Effectiveness in Technology-Mediated Distance Learning. *Academy of Management Journal*, 40(6), 1282-1309.

Whalen, T. & Wright, D. (1998). Distance Training in the Virtual Workplace. In M. Igbaria, M. Tan. (Eds.). *The Virtual Workplace.* Hershey, PA: Idea Group Publishing.

Williams, F., Rice, R. E. & Rogers, E. M. (1988). *Research Methods and the New Media.* New York: The Free Press.

Appendices

APPENDIX A

DATA INPUT FORMS

A-1. Course Information Form

Course ID	
Course Name	
Instructor's name	
Instructor POC info	
Course frequency per year	
Length of course (instructional hours)	
Average class size	
Learner throughput	

A-2. Course DL Screening Form

Add up the "yes" and "no" points in each column. Add them together and use the resulting number to interpret as follows:

0, negative values=DL is not suitable
1-3=DL may not be suitable; consider using technology insertion
4-6=Consider combined delivery
7+=DL is highly suitable

Course ID:	
VARIABLE	**Yes -1 No +1**
Hands-on activities essential	
Specialized tools or equipment is required	
Group training in functional teams is required	
Group problem solving is required	
Continuous feedback from instructor required	
Instructor-guided discussion required	
Group discussions are conducted	
Other requirement for physical presence of instructor and student	
Learner performance data required	
Learning objectives involve physical risk to student *[reverse code: yes=1, no= -1]*	

A-3 Instructional Unit Form

List all instructional units in the course, with the following information.

Course ID:					
Instructional unit	# of hrs	Instructional activities [1]	Type of learning objective [2]	How objective assessed [3]	Media choices[4]

Instructional unit: a group of lessons or modules that are integrated to complete a usable skill, knowledge, or to aid in scheduling a course. An instructional unit is a basic component of courses, and when developed or converted into a learning module for DL delivery, it is the basic unit of reuse that can be combined, integrated, or re-scheduled in a course.

[1]*Instructional activities:*
1=lecture
2=question & answer
3=instructor demo
4=instructor-guided discussions
5=student group activity
6=hands-on activity

[2]*Learning objective types:*
1=Cognitive
2= Software
3=Problem solving
4=Affective
5=Psychomotor

[3]*Assessment types:*
1=multiple choice
2=fill-in-blanks
3=short answer
4=essay questions
5=topical/research paper
6= individual project
7=oral presentation
8=group project

[4]*Appropriate media choices:*
1=CBT/CAI
2=WBT
3=TC
4=VTT or videotape
5=CBT/WBT

APPENDIX B

DEFINITIONS

Source: adapted from Landon, Bruce, 1998 at http://www.ctt.cb.ca/landonline/glossary.html.

Accessibility - for persons with disabilities entails providing for a universal text version without relying on frames, tables, or images.

Analyzing and tracking - facilities for statistical analysis of student-related data; the ability to display the progress of individual students in the course structure.

Apple Server - an Internet server running the Apple Computer Operating System.

Application sharing - the ability to run an application on one machine and share the window view across the Web. May also include provisions for sharing mouse control of the application.

Asynchronous sharing - the exchange of data and files where the correspondents are not online at the same time.

Authorization tools - tools that assign access and other privileges to specific users or user groups.

BBS file exchange (Bulletin Board Service) - facility for downloading files and uploading\posting files over the Web.

Bookmarks - Bookmarks identify Internet locations. This category covers the creation, display, management and updating of bookmarks.

Building motivation - facilities for self-help (and possibly other help such as a "buddy system") to provide encouragement and enhance morale.

Building knowledge - facilities to accumulate and share the knowledge gained by individual instructors through their experience with distance education. Examples range from simple Q&A files to extensive database style data warehouses of tips, workarounds, and class exercises.

Chat - a feature that allows the exchange of text (e.g., Internet Relay Chat).

Client Platform - the program on the users machine that allows it to interact with the server, usually a browser or a proprietary program specific to the server application.

Client - Client tool installation includes both the student client and the instructor client software.

Course managing - facilities to enable instructors to collect information from or about students related to their progress in the course structure also to permit/deny access to course resources.

Course monitoring - facilities that provide information about the usage of course resources by individual students and groups of students.

Course tools - instructor tasks related to bringing course materials together and managing the student's use/access of those materials.

Course planning - tools that enable at least initial course layout and or structuring.

Crash recovery tools - facilities to recover from communications or server hardware failure without loss of data (in addition to the tools provided by the operating system).

Customize settings - the ability to reconfigure menus, command buttons, and other features of the product to suit an individual user.

Data tools - tools for marking online, managing records, analyzing and tracking.

Disk Space - the amount of hard disk storage space required for the program to operate.

E-mail - Electronic Mail using the Internet protocols (unless otherwise indicated).

Ease of use - the "naturalness" of the interface for the task at hand and the training required to be able to use the product.

Exit Considerations - factors that are only important when changing from one application to another, these often involve translating data from a proprietary format to a common format so that the new application can read the data from the old application.

Exporting - sending/uploading files or data from the product to other applications/products.

Extra Considerations - information or restrictions beyond the evaluation criteria category scheme.

Group browsing - a group tour of Web sites with a shared browser window; some interaction capability between the members of the group and the tour leader.

Help desk tools - tools that assist the technical administration personnel in handling trouble calls and requests for technical assistance.

Hits Rank - the rank order of the number of times a page is accessed or relative popularity.

Importing - bringing/loading in of files or data from outside the product.

Integration - The part of the application design that facilitates efficient (seamless) transition between tasks and/or modules using the same user interface.

Installation tools- facilities that are used in the initial setup of the application or in upgrading from a previous version.

Instructor Tools - facilities primarily intended for use by instructors, markers and course designers.

Instructor support tools - facilities to assist technical support personnel in providing technical assistance to instructors using the application.

Instructional designing - facilities to help instructors create learning sequences.

Learner tools - Tools/facilities used by the student learner at their location, the client side of distance education.

Lesson tools - tools that facilitate the development and deployment of instructional sequences smaller than a whole course, like assignments, modules, topics, etc.

Limitations of package - capacities and restrictions on the usage of the application software.

Managing records - facilities for organizing and keeping track of course-related information.

Marking online - facilities that support the marking of student generated material while online.

Minimum Level - lowest level of browser that can be used with the application. level1 is text only browser, level2 is equivalent to Netscape 2.0, level3 is equivalent to Netscape 3.0, level4 is equivalent to Netscape 4.0 etc.

Motivation building - self-help tools and other facilities that provide direct encouragement to overcome difficulties that impede or impair student performance.

Multimedia - support for images, audio, video, and VRML files.

Navigation - the menu, command button, and right-click context menus that enable program functions.

Newsgroups - Newsgroups facility includes Usenet newsgroups and like functions.

Number - limits on the available resources determined by the software capacities or the license.

On-going Cost - continuing year to year application costs for licensing, service contracts, etc. beyond the start-up cost.

Openness - the extensibility of the interface to enable additional functions to be added such as with a macro facility, also the use of "open standards" versus proprietary formats for data and control.

Options - features of the application that are not necessary, but perhaps desirable add-ons to the basic package.

Other efficiencies - refers to the operating delays occasioned when switching from another task to the product or delays from the repetitive tasks such as many layers of menus without shortcut keys.

Other Limitations - limitations that stem from the application software situation such as version number where higher numbers usually indicate more mature (less buggy) software.

Presenting information - facilities for formatting, displaying, or showing course material over the Web.

Pricing - list price of the application software package varies among vendors in part because the pricing models are different.

Progress tracking - student's ability to check marks on assignments and tests.

RAM - random access memory usually specified in KB (kilobytes) or MB (megabytes).

Rapid course revising - the ability to change the structure of the course and its assignments, exams, etc.

Remote access tools - tools for application system administration from more than one machine.

Resource tools - tools for building knowledge, team building, and building motivation among instructors.

Resource monitoring - the ability to display the disk space and CPU resources devoted to the application while it is being used.

Security tools - tools to prevent unauthorized access and/or modification of data. Includes a wide range of approaches and methods.

Security - Browser security refers to the support for secure transactions on the Web and to verify the security of downloaded code.

Self-assessing - facilities for self-assessment such as practice quizzes and other survey style assessment tools that may or may not be scored online.

Server Platform - the operating system of the Internet server machine.

Stability of interface - refers to the sameness of the interface that enables experienced users to continue using the interface in their accustomed ways in the context of upgrades and changes to the supporting software.

Startup - the task delay occasioned when using the function for the first time in a session.

Start-up Cost - initial cost of acquiring the application and getting it running locally.

Student tools - applications that cater to the special needs of telelearners.

Student support tools - tools that facilitate the tasks of an operator responding to requests for help by student users of the application.

Study skill building - Study skill building includes facilities that support effective study practices, which can range form simple review tools to mini courses in how to study.

System tools - authorization tools, security tools, resource monitoring tools, remote access tools, and crash recovery tools.

Target Level - level of browser that was intended to work best with the application. level1 is text only browser, level2 is equivalent to Netscape 2.0, level3 is equivalent to Netscape 3.0, level4 is equivalent to Netscape 4.0 etc.

Team building - the ability of instructors with common interests to communicate in a way that facilitates their forming a sense of group/team identity.

Technical admin tools - the setup and maintenance tasks involved on the server side of the application and extending to setup/configuration of client side software to work properly with the server side application (some of these tasks may be carried out by instructors in some situations).

Technical Support - customer service for technical administrators usually from the application vendor.

Teleconferencing - audio conferencing.

Testing - facilities to assist in the making up of practice quizzes, tests, exams, and other assignments.

Time efficiency - the speed of loading and using the product in the context of other concurrent tasks.

Unix Server - Unix server operating system software, sometimes customized to a specific hardware vendor i.e. Solaris for Sun Servers.

Videoconferencing - broadcasting video to users without a video input device.

Virtual space - MOOs, MUDs, and virtual meeting rooms.

Web Browsing - Tools for viewing HTML documents (also see Browsers)

Whiteboard - a shared text window that may also support shared drawing.

WindowsNT 4.0 Server - Microsoft Windows NT version 4.0 server operating system software (version 5.0 was recently renamed Windows 2000).

APPENDIX C

Infrastructure Survey and Upgrade Requirements

INTERNET REQUIREMENTS	Instructor/learner upgrades required
Internet connectivity? • Asynchronous capability • Synchronous capability	Need Internet connectivity for WBT. For synchronous requirements, need access to chat facilities, shared application server (e.g., Microsoft NetMeeting).
How accessible is this connectivity? • Always available • Available 80% of time • Available 65% of time • Less than 50% availability	If available <65% of the time, need more Internet connections.
How will connectivity be achieved? • Modem /dial up • LAN • WAN	Need reliable access for use through WAN, LAN, or dial up connection. LAN/WAN connectivity is faster and preferable. If dial up connectivity is used, minimum speed required (at both ends) is 28.8 KBPS for asynchronous WBT, but 56 KBPS is preferred. For synchronous WBT, a higher speed LAN/WAN connection is preferred, and 56 KBPS is a minimum.
How fast is the speed of connectivity? • 28.8Kb • 56Kb • 128Kb • 256Kb • 1.5 Mb (T-1) • 155 Mb (OC-3 / DS-3)	
Is Internet connectivity provided through a shared facility?	If Internet connectivity is provided through a shared Internet gateway, then aggregate throughput (total bandwidth of the "pipe" or gateway to the Internet) should be adequate to serve users during peak usage times.
Do you have an Internet e-mail account?	All instructors and learners should have an Internet e-mail account.
DESKTOP/LAN	**Instructor upgrades required**
Is your desktop connected to an LAN?	Instructors need access to shared resources on the LAN; students may need access to download CBT files or for access to the Internet.
Do you have access to a shared file server?	Instructional content can be stored in sub-directories on a shared file server for use by multiple instructors.
Do you have a web browser loaded on your desktop?	All PCs used in the DL environment should have a standard browser loaded for use.
Are web plug-ins allowed on your workstation? • Java • Shockwave • Adobe Acrobat • Real Audio	If plug-ins are not allowed to be installed, this will severely limit the types of learning content (and methods) by which the content can be delivered to the desktop. For example, Shockwave segments large courseware applications into small chunks that can then be played on the workstation.
What office productivity software do you have access to? • Lotus Suite • Microsoft Office	Most office suites have the capability to save documents in HTML format and to create hyperlinks to Internet documents.
What graphics packages do you use?	Most graphics packages have some ability to save graphics in multiple formats for use in web pages.
What type of desktop hardware do you have? • 486 (<150 MHz) • Pentium I (150-300 MHz) • Pentium II (300+ MHz)	It is highly unlikely that a workstation with less than 150 MHz processing speed will be adequate for DL delivery, and even less so for courseware development.
What is the storage capacity of your desktop? • <5 GB • 5 or more GB	Multimedia files (even if downloaded temporarily) are very large, so adequate storage must be available on the desktop. A minimum of 5 GB is required to run courseware at the desktop. An exception to this would be a completely web-based course that does not require any downloading of large multimedia files to the desktop.

APPENDIX D

ON-LINE RESOURCES FOR DISTANCE LEARNING

Overview

A large number of universities and commercial organizations offer some form of distance learning. This appendix contains a non-exhaustive list of Web sites that offer discussions of distance learning issues and concepts, Web sites that are themselves distance learning environments, or Web sites that have been listed somewhere else in the book for distance learning course development. The list is current as of the last quarter of 1999. The authors and the publisher of this book have no involvement or control over the quality or accuracy of the information provided by these Web sites.

Course Management Systems

Asymmetrix Toolbook
http://www.asymetrix.com/

Course Info and Campus
http://product.blackboard.net/courseinfo/

LearningSpace
http://www.lotus.com/home.nsf/tabs/learnspace
Also: IBM Global Campus at http://www.ibm.com

Saba Software
http://www.saba.com

TopClass Server
http://www.wbtsystems.com/

Web Course in a Box
http://www.madduck.com/index.html

WebCT
http://homebrew1.cs.ubc.ca/webct/

WebMentor
> *http://www.avilar.com/*

Web Development Tools

HTML Converters

WWW Consortium site
> *http://www.w3.org/Tools/Word_proc_filers.html*

Yahoo
> *http://dir.yahoo.com/Computers_and_Internet/Software/Internet/*
World_Wide_Web/HTML_Converters

HTML Editors

Yahoo
> *http://dir.yahoo.com/Computers_and_Internet/Software/Reviews/*
> *Titles/Internet/Web_Authoring_Tools/HTML_Editors/*

Communication Tools

Audio Conferencing

Netscape's CoolTalk
> *http://home.netscape.com/navigator/v3.0/cooltalk.html*

CHAT Systems

FreeChat
> *http://www.sonic.net/~nbs/unix/www/freechat/*

IChat
> *http://www.ichat.com/*

Conferencing Systems

ConferWeb (MacIntosh)
> *http://www.caup.washington.edu/software/conferweb/*

CoW (UNIX)
> *http://calypso.rs.itd.umich.edu/COW/*

Dialogue (Windows)
> *http://www.magictree.com/*

Desktop Video Conferencing Packages

CU-SeeMe
> *http://www.wpine.com/*

NetMeeting®
> *http://www.microsoft.com/netmeeting/*

Electronic Mail Packages

Eudora Light
> *http://www.eudora.com/*

Multimedia Tools

3D Modeling Tools

Specular's Infini-D((MacIntosh)
> *http://www.zutroy.com/Infini-D/links.html*

Template Graphic's 3Space Publisher((PC)
> *http://www.tgs.com*

Action Recorder Software

Lotus ScreenCam®
> *http://www.lotus.com/home.nsf/welcome/screencam/*

Microsoft's DirectShow®
> *http://www.microsoft.com/directx/overview/dshow/*

Audio File Formats and Editing Tools

Microsoft Waveform (*.wav)
> *http://www.microsoft.com/*

NeXT/Sun Sparc's RealAudio (*.au)
> *http://www.real.com/*

SoundEdit 16
> *http://www.macromedia.com/*

Sound Forge
> *http://www.sonicfoundry.com/*

Image Editors

Adobe PhotoShop®
> *http://www.adobe.com*

Corel PhotoPaint®
> *http://www.corel.com*

Macromedia xRes®
> *http://www.macromedia.com/*

Object Oriented Image Editors

Adobe Illustrator®
> *http://www.adobe.com*

CorelDRAW(
> *http://www.corel.com*

Macromedia Freehand(®
> *http://www.macromedia.com*

MetaCreations Fractal Expression®
> *http://www.metacreations.com*

Distance Learning Offices, Institutes, or Centers

Center for Instructional Technology Information Resource Guides:
> *http://www.unc.edu/cit/guides/guides.html*

Virginia Polytechnic Institute and State University's CyberSchool
> *http://www.cyber.vt.edu/*

Examples of Distance Learning Courses or Programs

Infobahn Webschool
> *http://www.i-bahn.com/web/index.html*

List of Programs and Universities Offering Distance Learning Courses
> *http://dir.yahoo.com/Education/Distance_Learning/*

List of accredited Distance Learning Degrees
> *http://www.accrediteddldegrees.com/*

Virginia Tech Online
http://www.vto.vt.edu/classes.html

Virtual University for Small and Medium Sized Enterprises
http://www.vusme.org

On-Line Research Articles on Distance Learning

Special Issue of the Journal of Computer Mediated Communication
http://www.ascusc.org/jcmc/vol4/issue2/

The No Significant Difference Phenomenon by T. L. Russell (1996)
http://tenb.mta.ca/phenom/phenom1.html

Courses About Distance Learning

Graduate Certificate in Open and Distance Learning
http://www.usq.edu.au/material/course/us59

Virtual Learning Environments

Generation21 Learning Systems
http://www.gen21.com/

Other Distance Learning Resources

Distance Learning Statistics: National Center for Educational Statistics Report
http://nces.ed.gov/

Glossary of Distance Learning Terms by B. Landon
http://www.ctt.bc.ca/landonline/glossary.html

Microsoft in Higher Education
http://www.microsoft.com/education/hed/online/

PBS Adult Learning Service
http://www.pbs.org/adultlearning/als/

United States Distance Learning Association
http://www.usdla.org/

Virginia Tech On-Line Summer School 1998 Assessment Report by C. D. Taylor and S. R. Burnkrant
http://www.edtech.vt.edu/assess/ol_summer98

INDEX

About the Authors

FRANCE BELANGER.

France Belanger is an assistant professor of information systems in the Department of Accounting and Information Systems and a researcher for the Center for Global Electronic Commerce at Virginia Polytechnic Institute and State University.

Prior to her academic career, Dr. Belanger has held various technical, marketing and managerial positions in large information systems and telecommunications corporations in Canada. More recently, she has provided consulting services to corporations in Florida. Her research interests focus on the impacts of distributed communication technologies on organizations. She has conducted research and written about distributed work arrangements like telecommuting and the virtual organization; organizational uses of telecommunication technologies, in particular for electronic commerce; and, the role of technologies in organizational learning, in particular for distance education and training. She has presented her work at several national conferences and has published in *Information and Management, The Information Society: An International Journal, IEEE Transactions of Professional Communication* and the *Journal of Information Systems Education.*

DIANNE H. JORDAN

Dr. Jordan is a strategic information technology planner at Booz Allen & Hamilton, where she focuses on advanced distributed learning initiatives. She recently completed a strategic evaluation of over 1,000 technical training and education courses for the U.S. Air Force that included a media analysis, benefit/cost analysis, and infrastructure requirements analysis.

She has 20 years of professional experience in private industry, academia, and the federal government. She served as the CyberCongress Project Manager for the U.S. House of Representatives where she supervised the deployment of Web-based solutions for business units of the House. She was on the faculty at Baruch College (CUNY) where she taught telecommunications and the use of information technologies for strategic advantage. She has been a senior federal manager in the Department of Defense in the areas of data communications, operating systems software, information security, and office automation.

Dr. Jordan has a Ph.D. in Information Systems from the University of South Florida.